W9-ABG-151

R
726.2
.J37
2007

HEALTH CARE DIRECTIVES

by
Margaret C. Jasper

Oceana's Legal Almanac Series:
Law for the Layperson

Oceana Publications

 KVCC KALAMAZOO VALLEY COMMUNITY COLLEGE LIBRARY

APR 0 5 2007

Information contained in this work has been obtained by Oceana Publications from sources believed to be reliable. However, neither the Publisher nor its authors guarantee the accuracy or completeness of any information published herein, and neither the Publisher nor its authors shall be responsible for any errors, omissions or damages arising from the use of this information. This work is published with the understanding that the Publisher and its authors are supplying information, but are not attempting to render legal or other professional services. If such services are required, the assistance of an appropriate professional should be sought.

You may order this or any other Oxford University Press publication by visiting the Oxford University Press and Oceana websites at www.oup.com and www.oceanalaw.com respectively.

Library of Congress Control Number: 2006935506

ISBN 978-0-19-532364-1

Oceana's Legal Almanac Series: Law for the Layperson
ISSN 1075-7376

©2007 Oxford University Press, Inc.

All rights reserved. No part of this publication may be reproduced or transmitted in any form or by any means, electronic or mechanical, including photocopy, recording, xerography, or any information storage and retrieval system, without permission in writing from the publisher.

Manufactured in the United States of America on acid-free paper.

To My Husband Chris

Your love and support
are my motivation and inspiration

-and-

In memory of my son, Jimmy

Table of Contents

ABOUT THE AUTHOR

MARGARET C. JASPER is an attorney engaged in the general practice of law in South Salem, New York, concentrating in the areas of personal injury and entertainment law. Ms. Jasper holds a Juris Doctor degree from Pace University School of Law, White Plains, New York, is a member of the New York and Connecticut bars, and is certified to practice before the United States District Courts for the Southern and Eastern Districts of New York, the United States Court of Appeals for the Second Circuit, and the United States Supreme Court.

Ms. Jasper has been appointed to the law guardian panel for the Family Court of the State of New York, is a member of a number of professional organizations and associations, and is a New York State licensed real estate broker operating as Jasper Real Estate, in South Salem, New York.

Margaret Jasper maintains a website at http://www.JasperLawOffice.com.

In 2004, Ms. Jasper successfully argued a case before the New York Court of Appeals that gave mothers of babies who are stillborn due to medical negligence the right to bring a legal action and recover emotional distress damages. This successful appeal overturned a 26-year-old New York case precedent that previously prevented mothers of stillborn babies from suing their negligent medical providers.

Ms. Jasper is the author and general editor of the following legal almanacs:

AIDS Law
The Americans with Disabilities Act
Animal Rights Law
Auto Leasing
Bankruptcy Law for the Individual Debtor
Banks and their Customers
Becoming a Citizen
Buying and Selling Your Home

Commercial Law
Consumer Rights Law
Co-ops and Condominiums: Your Rights and Obligations as Owner
Copyright Law
Credit Cards and the Law
Custodial Rights
Dealing with Debt
Dictionary of Selected Legal Terms
Drunk Driving Law
DWI, DUI and the Law
Education Law
Elder Law
Employee Rights in the Workplace
Employment Discrimination Under Title VII
Environmental Law
Estate Planning
Everyday Legal Forms
Executors and Personal Representatives: Rights and
    Responsibilities
Harassment in the Workplace
Health Care and Your Rights
Health Care Directives
Hiring Household Help and Contractors: Your Rights and Obliga-
    tions Under the Law
Home Mortgage Law Primer
Hospital Liability Law
How To Change Your Name
How To Protect Your Challenged Child
How To Start Your Own Business
Identity Theft and How To Protect Yourself
Individual Bankruptcy and Restructuring
Injured on the Job: Employee Rights, Worker's Compensation and
    Disability Insurance Law
International Adoption
Juvenile Justice and Children's Law
Labor Law
Landlord-Tenant Law
Law for the Small Business Owner
The Law of Attachment and Garnishment
The Law of Buying and Selling
The Law of Capital Punishment
The Law of Child Custody
The Law of Contracts
The Law of Debt Collection

The Law of Dispute Resolution
The Law of Immigration
The Law of Libel and Slander
The Law of Medical Malpractice
The Law of No-Fault Insurance
The Law of Obscenity and Pornography
The Law of Personal Injury
The Law of Premises Liability
The Law of Product Liability
The Law of Speech and the First Amendment
The Law of Violence Against Women
Lemon Laws
Living Together: Practical Legal Issues
Living Wills
Marriage and Divorce
Missing and Exploited Children: How to Protect Your Child
Motor Vehicle Law
Nursing Home Negligence
Patent Law
Pet Law
Prescription Drugs
Privacy and the Internet: Your Rights and Expectations Under the Law
Probate Law
Real Estate Law for the Homeowner and Broker
Religion and the Law
Retirement Planning
The Right to Die
Rights of Single Parents
Small Claims Court
Social Security Law
Special Education Law
Teenagers and Substance Abuse
Trademark Law
Trouble Next Door: What to do With Your Neighbor
Victim's Rights Law
Welfare: Your Rights and the Law
What if It Happened to You: Violent Crimes and Victims' Rights
What if the Product Doesn't Work: Warranties & Guarantees
Workers' Compensation Law
Your Child's Legal Rights: An Overview
Your Rights in a Class Action Suit
Your Rights as a Tenant
Your Rights Under the Family and Medical Leave Act
You've Been Fired: Your Rights and Remedies

INTRODUCTION

This almanac discusses the topic of health care directives and the patient's right to participate in their own health care decisions. A living will and a durable power of attorney for health care are examples of important health care directives. A living will allows you to make your health care decisions ahead of time should you become incapacitated. A durable power of attorney for health care enables you to appoint someone to make sure your wishes are carried out if you become unable to make your own health care decisions. You can also leave instructions regarding your funeral and burial arrangements, which eases the decision-making burden often left to the family.

The patient's right to refuse medical treatment is examined, including advance medical directives, health care proxies, do not resuscitate orders, and the patient's right to pain management. Legal issues concerning a medical provider's failure to carry out a patient's wishes are also discussed. Additional topics include religious objections to executing a living will, capacity issues such as age and mental competence, informed consent, right-to-die legislation, and prohibitions against assisted suicide.

The Appendix provides applicable statutes, resource directories, and other pertinent information and data. The Glossary contains definitions of many of the terms used throughout the almanac.

CHAPTER 1:
THE PATIENT'S RIGHT TO PARTICIPATE IN HEALTH CARE DECISIONS

IN GENERAL

An important part of planning for your future is recognizing that health concerns may arise that require you to explore options and make extremely important life and death decisions. Every person has the right and responsibility to fully participate in all decisions related to their health care, including the right to refuse treatment.

If there comes a point, however, that you are no longer able to make those important decisions—e.g., due to mental or physical incapacity—it is important to make sure that those decisions are made for you by those you trust will act in your best interests, and according to your wishes.

CAPACITY

In relation to end-of-life decision-making, a patient has medical decision-making capacity if he or she has the ability to understand the medical problem and the risks and benefits of the available treatment options. The term "capacity" is frequently used interchangeably with "competency" but is not the same.

Competency is a legal status imposed by the court. For example, minors are deemed legally incompetent to make decisions concerning their right to forego medical treatment.

A few states require clear and convincing evidence that an incompetent patient would want to refuse life-support before treatment may be stopped unless the patient has completed an advance directive authorized by the state's law.

THE PATIENT'S RIGHT TO REFUSE MEDICAL TREATMENT

As set forth below, an individual has a constitutional right to request the withdrawal or withholding of medical treatment, including the cessation of food and water, even if doing so will result in the person's death. Honoring a person's right to refuse medical treatment or other life sustaining intervention, especially at the end of life, is the most widely practiced and widely accepted "right to die" policy in our society.

The American Medical Association Statement on Withholding or Withdrawing of Life-Prolonging Medical Treatment is set forth at Appendix 1 of this almanac.

The Patient's Right to Refuse Life-Sustaining Treatment

A life-sustaining treatment has been defined to include any medical treatment, procedure, or intervention that, in the judgment of the attending physician, when applied to the patient, would serve only to prolong the dying process where the patient has a terminal illness or injury, or would serve only to maintain the patient in a condition of permanent unconsciousness.

Patients have the right to stop not only commonly recognized life-sustaining measures, such as assisted ventilation and cardiopulmonary resuscitation (CPR), but to also discontinue any other medical treatments that may prolong life, such as kidney dialysis, surgical procedures, blood transfusions, heart medication, antibiotics, etc., regardless of whether the refusal may result in death.

Nevertheless, life-sustaining treatment does not include symptomatic treatment, including the administration of medication or the performance of any medical treatment where, in the opinion of the attending physician, the medication or treatment is necessary to provide comfort or to alleviate pain, even if the pain medication has the effect of hastening their death. A patient's right to pain management is discussed below.

The Patient's Right to Refuse Nutrition and Hydration

Artificially provided nutrition and hydration refers to a medical treatment consisting of the administration of food and water through a tube or intravenous line, where the recipient is not required to chew or swallow voluntarily. Artificially provided nutrition and hydration does not include assisted feeding, such as spoon or bottle-feeding.

Do Not Resuscitate Order

A Do-Not-Resuscitate Order (DNR) is a physician's written order instructing health care providers not to attempt cardiopulmonary resuscitation (CPR) in the event the patient suffers cardiac or respiratory arrest. A person with a valid DNR order will not be given CPR under these circumstances. Although the DNR order is written at the request of a person or his or her family, it generally must be signed by a physician to be valid. A non-hospital DNR order is written for individuals who are at home and do not want to receive CPR.

Prior to issuing a DNR order, the patient's attending physician must provide certain information to the patient, or to the surrogate, concerning the patient's condition, including:

1. The patient's diagnosis and prognosis;

2. The reasonably foreseeable risks and benefits of CPR; and

3. The consequences of a DNR order.

If the attending physician objects to the issuance of a DNR order, he or she must inform the patient or surrogate of that objection, and make arrangements to transfer the patient to another physician who will comply with the patient's directive.

A sample Do Not Resuscitate Order is set forth at Appendix 2 of this almanac.

Benefits and Burdens Assessment

Benefits and burdens refers to a commonly used guideline for deciding whether or not to withhold or withdraw medical treatments. A benefit refers to the successful outcome of a medical procedure or treatment. The outcome can be medical, functional, or support the patient's values.

An example of a successful medical outcome is the ability to get the patient's heart beating again after he or she goes into cardiac arrest. An example of a successful functional outcome is when a person is able to write again after having a stroke that affected his or her dominant hand. Finally, a successful outcome that supports the patient's values is the fulfilment of a patient's dying wish, such as the ability to die at home.

Nevertheless, a benefit may be seen as a burden under certain circumstances. For example, a doctor may view resuscitation as a benefit, whereas the patient may consider it a burden if it serves to extend his or her suffering. Thus, there should be a careful and thorough discussion of the benefits and burdens of various treatment plans with the patient and the patient's family members and representatives.

Most states acknowledge that a competent adult has the legal right to refuse medical care. On the other hand, many states also set forth certain policy concerns—such as preservation of life and suicide prevention—to limit this right. The courts have looked to the circumstances concerning the patient when denial of the patient's rights are put in issue.

Generally, if the patient is capable of recovery, the state's interest in preserving life has more merit than when the patient is on his or her death bed with no possibility of recovery. Further, the courts have distinguished between the act of suicide and the patient's right to die a natural death without being placed on life support.

States have also expressed concern over the impact refusal of medical treatment will have on innocent third parties—in particular, minor children. For example, certain religious groups hold that medical treatment—e.g., blood transfusions—violates their religious beliefs. In these cases, the courts have generally held that a competent adult, without dependent children, may refuse treatment. However, if the refusal to have a critical blood transfusion will cause a single mother to die and leave her children orphaned, the court will likely order the parent to undergo the treatment. The court will also usually order a pregnant woman to undergo treatment that is necessary to protect the unborn child.

Thus, where there is an overriding state concern, such as the protection of third parties, the adult may be compelled to accept the treatment.

A health care provider—e.g., on moral grounds—may not be able to accept the patient's wishes to forego necessary treatment. In that case, the health care provider should assist the patient in locating a health care provider who is able to care for the patient according to his or her wishes.

Some health care providers have raised concerns that withholding treatment is tantamount to abandonment. However, the courts have generally held that where treatment would be futile, terminating or withholding treatment is not abandonment.

Minors

Because minors are deemed legally incompetent to make decisions concerning their right to forego medical treatment, the minor's parents make the decisions on the minor's behalf. However, when a minor is in critical need of treatment but the parent—e.g., due to religious beliefs—will not consent, court orders are routinely granted to the health care provider to administer the treatment. In some cases, a guardian is appointed by the court to protect the child.

A health care provider who is faced with a life-threatening situation must render the necessary treatment to the minor despite the parent's wishes, and instruct the parents to obtain a court order immediately if they want to prevent such treatment.

In situations where the minor is in such a physical state that any attempt to sustain life would be futile and cruel, the courts have held that the parents and health care provider can mutually decide to withhold treatment without seeking a court order. Nevertheless, this law generally does not permit the withholding of food and water as a means to hasten death in the case of a minor.

Release From Liability

Most hospitals will require a patient, or his or her representative, to sign a document which releases the attending physician, the hospital and its employees from liability if treatment is withheld or withdrawn. The document generally states the circumstances of the patient's condition, e.g., brain death, etc., giving rise to the request to terminate treatment.

The release of liability document also references the patient's advance directives—e.g., the patient's living will and durable power of attorney for health care—as proof of the patient's desire to forego life sustaining procedures and his or her appointment of an agent to make this decision if he or she is unable to do so.

In a subsequent medical malpractice action, a defendant may set forth a defense alleging that the patient assumed the risk of non-treatment by virtue of the release of liability. Nevertheless, a release from liability would not limit a health care provider's liability for negligence. If the release contained such a provision, it would likely be unenforceable on public policy grounds.

A sample release from liability is set forth at Appendix 3 of this almanac.

THE PATIENT'S RIGHT TO PAIN MANAGEMENT

People who experience pain have the right to receive treatment to alleviate their pain even if the pain medication has the effect of hastening their death. Proper treatment of pain depends on the type, location and duration of the pain. Efforts to reduce or eliminate the pain may include evaluation and treatment by surgeons or other doctors who specialize in treating the part of the body that is believed to be the source of the pain.

Classification of Pain

In general, there are three classifications of pain:

1. Acute Pain—Acute pain is usually severe and lasts for short periods of time. It can come from an accident, the onset of illness or disease, or as a result of surgery. Usually, the pain indicates that the body's tissue has been injured. Acute pain usually disappears as healing occurs.

2. Chronic Pain—Chronic pain stays for a long period of time. Chronic pain often accompanies certain diseases and conditions such as arthritis, migraine headaches, cancer, or sensitivity from an old injury or surgery.

3. Intractable Pain—Intractable pain occurs because the cause of the pain cannot be removed or otherwise treated. Intractable pain remains even after reasonable efforts have been made to reduce or eliminate it.

Responsibilities of the Health Care Provider in Managing Pain

In order to properly understand the patient's condition and treat their pain, the health care provider should:

1. Perform a physical exam and take a history of the patient's condition.

2. Conduct any tests needed to determine the source of the pain.

3. Coordinate the patient's care with any other health care providers who are treating the patient.

4. Refer the patient to a specialist who has experience treating people with pain.

The Patient's Right to Information

People experiencing pain have the right to be advised as to:

1. The complete and current information about their condition;

2. The range of appropriate treatment options; and

3. The prognosis for their condition.

In addition, people experiencing pain are entitled to participate fully in the decisions affecting their care, and give truly informed consent to the treatment plan their doctor recommends. Regardless of the recommended treatment, the health care provider is also required to advise the patient of the risks and benefits of all available treatments, and the goals of treatment.

People in pain have the right to receive treatment for their pain. Pain treatment may involve the use of drug and non-drug therapies, often in combination. These may include:

1. Temporary relief, such as ibuprofen and aspirin and other "over-the-counter" medications for mild to moderate acute pain.

2. Prescription pain relievers, such as anti-inflammatory drugs or opiates to manage moderate to severe pain.

3. Physical therapy or lifestyle changes.

In addition, patients have the right to choose alternative treatments to manage their pain, including physical therapy, acupuncture, biofeedback/relaxation techniques, massage, chiropractic care, psychotherapy to help manage depression that may accompany chronic or intractable pain, hypnosis, and behavior modification.

Narcotic Treatment for Pain

After evaluating the patient's condition, the health care provider may prescribe stronger medication, such as anti-depressants, nerve block injections, or opiates. Opiates, also known as narcotics, include morphine, codeine, and percodan. If the doctor will not prescribe opiates, the patient has the right to be referred to a doctor who will prescribe this pain medication.

Medical Marijuana

There has been much controversy about the legalization of smoked marijuana for medical purposes. One marijuana-based product, Marinol, which is the synthetic oral form of the major active ingredient in marijuana, has been approved since 1985 for the treatment of nausea and vomiting associated with cancer chemotherapy, and the FDA subsequently approved its use in loss of appetite and weight loss problems related to AIDS.

Since 1986, Marinol had been classified by the Drug Enforcement Agency (DEA) as a Schedule II drug, which placed certain restrictions on prescribing the drug. In July 1999, in accord with the scientific and medical evaluation and recommendations of HHS, the DEA lowered Marinol to a Schedule III drug. This reclassification makes the drug more available to patients, and allows physicians to write prescriptions providing as many as five refills within six months.

Approval of marijuana for medical purposes requires the same level of scientific evidence required for all other pharmaceutical products. The National Institutes of Health (NIH), a department of the Department of Health and Human Services (HHS), and the Institute of Medicine (IOM) have both conducted reviews of existing research on the possible medical effectiveness of smoked marijuana. Although both reviews have concluded that research obtained thus far has not demonstrated a therapeutic benefit, the reviews also concluded that further research was justified, especially for certain diseases.

Although the IOM study found that some chemical components of marijuana show promise for therapeutic use, it is the delivery system—i.e., smoking—that presents health risks, thus, they have called for a study of alternative delivery methods of the beneficial components of marijuana.

In order to carry out additional scientific research, HHS has created a special process that enables them to provide research grade marijuana for non-NIH funded projects found to have scientific merit, after they have obtained permission from the Drug Enforcement Agency (DEA) and an Investigational New Drug (IND) license from the Food and Drug Administration (FDA).

In addition, the DEA has registered seven research initiatives to continue researching the effects of smoked marijuana as medicine. For example, under one program established by the State of California, researchers are studying the potential use of marijuana and its ingredients on conditions such as multiple sclerosis and pain. At this time, however, neither the medical community nor the scientific community has found sufficient data to conclude that smoked marijuana is the best approach to dealing with these important medical issues.

In the meantime, the DEA is working with pain management groups, such as Last Acts, to make sure that those who need access to safe, effective pain medication can get the best medication available.

INFORMED CONSENT

Along with a patient's right to participate in decisions about their health care is their right to understand what they are being told about their care and treatment. For example, the patient is entitled to a clear explanation of prescribed drugs, tests, treatments, and medical procedures.

The term "informed consent" refers to the requirement that a patient be apprised of the nature and risks of a medical procedure before the medical provider can validly claim exemption from liability for battery, or from responsibility for medical complications. Under the law, a health care provider cannot commence a medical procedure without first obtaining a patient's informed consent.

A sample informed consent agreement is set forth at Appendix 4 of this almanac.

Manner of Consent

A patient gives consent to medical treatment either by (1) express consent or (2) implied consent.

Express Consent

Express consent is obtained either in writing or orally. The health care provider is required to fully disclose all of the known and significant facts relevant to the procedure, in layperson's language, so that the patient can make an intelligent decision as to whether to go forward with the treatment.

For people with special needs, such as a hearing or vision disability, or the inability to understanding English, medical facilities must make skilled interpreters available to patients to explain and answer questions about their rights and provide information on how they can protect those rights. Translations and/or transcriptions of important forms, instructions and information must be provided if the patient requires them for an understanding of the documents.

Required Information

The following information should be provided to the patient to satisfy the informed consent requirement:

1. The diagnosis of the patient's condition and the prognosis without the proposed treatment;

2. The nature of the proposed treatment;

3. The goal to be achieved by the proposed treatment and the chance that the treatment will be successful;

4. The risks of the proposed treatment;

5. Any alternative treatments to the proposed treatment;

6. Identify:

(a) The health care provider(s) who discussed the proposed treatment with the patient;

(b) The health care provider(s) who will perform the proposed treatment;

7. Obtain consent to deviate from the proposed treatment in case of unforeseen circumstances.

8. Obtain consent to dispose of any tissue, organs or other body parts, if needed, for pathological study or research;

9. Acknowledgement that the patient's questions were fully discussed and adequately answered.

10. The patient's and/or legal guardian's signature, the signature of a witness, and the date, time, and location that the consent form was signed. If the patient is a minor, the parents may consent to the procedure, or, in the case of divorce, it is usually the parent having legal custody who may consent.

Where the health care provider has failed to obtain such consent, or where the quality of the consent is challenged, the patient may claim lack of informed consent for the procedure unless consent can be implied, as set forth below.

Implied Consent

Implied consent is obtained, for example, when a patient submits to a simple procedure. However, there is no implied consent where the procedure is invasive or non-customary.

Further, once a surgeon begins an internal surgical procedure, there is a presumption of implied consent if the surgeon does other necessary procedures in the process. This is so even if there are relatives in the vicinity who may be consulted. This is because the surgeon is not permitted to leave the operating room, once the surgery has begun, to obtain consent.

However, such implied consent only applies to necessary procedures. If the procedure is elective, the surgeon has the duty to delay until he receives the necessary consent for the additional surgery.

Implied consent also applies in emergency situations. If the emergency involves risk to the patient's life, or the patient is unable to give consent due to unconsciousness, coma or other incapacity, it has been held that the patient would have consented to the treatment if he or she were able, thus consent is implied in such situations.

The existence of the emergency should be entered into the medical records, including the reason why the procedure was necessary, e.g., the patient's airway was blocked and an emergency tracheotomy was necessary or the patient would have choked to death.

Lack of Informed Consent

Lack of informed consent means that the patient did not fully understand what the health care provider was going to do, and was injured as a result of the health care provider's action. Further, the patient claims that if he had known what the health care provider planned to do, the patient would not have consented and, therefore, would have avoided the injury.

Absent an emergency, if the health care provider is able to ascertain, in advance of a surgical procedure, all of the possible alternatives available if an unexpected situation should arise during the operation, the patient should be informed of the alternatives and given the chance to decide if those alternatives are acceptable before the health care provider proceeds with the procedure.

Informed Consent and Prescription Drugs

More often than not, a patient is prescribed medication without any details given to them about the particular medication. They simply take the often illegibly handwritten prescription to the pharmacy, have it filled, and start taking the drug according to the label's directions. However, patients have the right to know much more about the medicines that they are taking, and should take advantage of those rights.

Most problems associated with prescription drugs occur because the patient did not receive enough information concerning the medicine to use it properly. For example, they are unaware of what side effects to expect, or they improperly mix the medication with a food or drink, or another medication. The improper use of prescription medications can be deadly.

It is important to ask your medical provider every question you may have concerning a medication that is prescribed for you. A patient has the right to be informed about all aspects of their medical treatment, including the risks and benefits of the medicines prescribed; the potential side effects; and the necessity of monitoring the medication's effects. The patient also has the right to know the results of any tests that demonstrate whether or not the medication is working. For example, if the medical provider prescribes a cholesterol-reducing drug, the patient should be advised whether or not the medication is effectively reducing their cholesterol level.

The patient should also discuss with their medical provider all of the medicines that they are presently taking, including over-the-counter medicines, and whether there are any concerns about the interaction between those medicines with the medicine being prescribed. In particular, a patient has the right to the following information:

1. The name of the medicine and how it is intended to treat the patient's condition;

2. The dosage, frequency and duration prescribed, and whether there are refills available;

3. The foods, drinks, and other medicines that may negatively interact with the medication being prescribed.

4. The potential side effects of the medicine, and instructions on how to proceed should the patient experience those side effects;

5. An explanation of any terms or directions the patient does not understand.

6. A copy of any written information that may be available concerning the medication they are being prescribed.

The Food and Drug Administration (FDA) provides updated information about medication errors, including specific drugs that have been confused with one another. The information has been compiled based on voluntary reports received from consumers, doctors and other clinicians, as well as mandatory reports from manufacturers. Information concerning medication errors is available from the FDA on-line at *http://www.fda.gov*.

RESPONSIBILITIES OF HEALTH CARE PROVIDERS

In order to ensure a patient's right and ability to participate in treatment decisions, health care providers should:

1. Provide patients with easily understood information and opportunity to decide among treatment options consistent with the informed consent process.

2. Discuss all treatment options with a patient in a culturally competent manner, including the option of no treatment at all.

3. Ensure that persons with disabilities have effective communications with members of the health system in making health care decisions.

4. Discuss all current treatments a patient may be undergoing, including those alternative treatments that are self-administered.

5. Discuss all risks, benefits, and consequences of treatment or nontreatment.

6. Give patients the opportunity to refuse treatment and to express preferences about future treatment decisions.

7. Discuss the use of advance directives—both living wills and durable powers of attorney for health care—with patients and their designated family members, as more fully discussed in Chapters 2 and 3 of this almanac.

8. Abide by the decisions made by the patient and/or the patient's designated representative consistent with the informed consent process.

CHAPTER 2:
WHAT IS AN ADVANCE DIRECTIVE?

IN GENERAL

An "advance directive" is a general term that refers to one's oral and written instructions about their future medical care, in the event that they become unconscious or too sick to express their intentions. Executing an advance directive gives an individual the opportunity to make his or her own end-of-life health care decisions long after he or she has lost the capacity to do so.

The opportunity to execute advance directives responds to the individual's wishes to have some control over his or her destiny. Advance directives respond to the individual's concern that medical technology will prolong their life long after any reasonable possibility of recovery has disappeared. Many people prefer to "die with dignity" rather than remain comatose in a hospital bed attached to life support equipment for an indefinite duration. Further, the emotional toll that such a scenario causes the patient's family is another important factor to be considered.

An advance directive authorizes the medical care provider to cease some or all of these life support measures. On the other hand, an advance directive may also be used to instruct the medical care provider to undertake certain life-sustaining treatments in certain defined circumstances. In short, it is about giving the patient the choice and the right to make these decisions.

Nevertheless, as discussed in Chapter 1, as long as the patient is able to express his or her own decisions, an advance directive will not be used and the patient has the right to accept or refuse any medical treatment regardless of the advance directive.

There has been an increasing interest in the topic of advance directives, largely because of the availability of changing medical technologies aimed at prolonging life. In addition, much publicized cases, such as the recent Schiavo case, discussed in Chapter 4 of this almanac, has pushed this issue to the forefront.

ADVANCE DIRECTIVES LEGISLATION

All 50 states and the District of Columbia have laws recognizing the patient's right to control his or her medical treatment, and the use of some type of advance directive. The availability and scope of the particular advance directive varies from state to state, therefore, the reader is advised to check the law of his or her jurisdiction for specific provisions. Thus far, no state has challenged an individual's advance health care directives, and many states have enacted statutes that explicitly allow advance directives.

In addition, case law has supported an individual's express wishes concerning end-of-life health care decisions. The problem arises when an individual has not expressed those wishes, in writing, leaving it to the court to decide, based on evidence, whether a patient would have wanted certain actions to be taken, such as removal of life support.

In order to make sure patients are aware of their rights to make their own end-of-life health care decisions, Congress enacted the *Patient Self Determination Act of 1990*, which requires hospitals to inform their patients about advance directives. The *Patient Self Determination Act* is discussed more fully in Chapter 5 of this almanac.

In addition, the National Conference of Commissioners on Uniform State Laws (NCCUSL), recognizing that there was inconsistency among state laws concerning the use of advance health care directives, drafted the *Health Care Decisions Act*. The Act is comprehensive and is designed to replace existing legislation concerning advance directives with one all-encompassing statute. The goal of the Act is to ensure that advance directives executed by a patient in one state will be followed if the patient is hospitalized in another state. The *Health Care Decisions Act* is discussed more fully in Chapter 6 of this almanac.

The only health care decisions that have thus far been outlawed in all states, except Oregon, concern assisted suicide and euthanasia, as more fully discussed in Chapter 7 of this almanac.

All states have some requirements for the execution of advance directives. For example, most states require witnesses to the signing and/or notarization. If there are any such formalities, you must make sure you follow them so that your advance directives will be followed. When choosing witnesses, you should not use people who are related to you; potential claimants to your estate, including heirs and persons named in your will; or your health care providers.

As set forth above, the law regarding advance directives varies from state to state. Therefore, if you spend a lot of time in another state, e.g., you own a second home out-of-state—you may consider executing an advance directive according to the laws of the second state. It is also advisable to name a different health care agent who is readily available in the second state, if the need arises, as your chosen health care agent should reside close to the location where you are being treated.

TYPES OF ADVANCE DIRECTIVES

As more fully discussed in Chapter 3, a living will and a durable power of attorney for health care are the two primary types of advance directives in use today. A living will is a document that contains your wishes concerning treatments you want or don't want administered if you are unable to express your wishes, e.g. due to incapacity. It usually only applies to end-of-life decisions. A durable power of attorney for health care, also known as a health care proxy, is a document that appoints someone to be your health care agent with the authority to make your health care decisions when you are unable to do so.

A comprehensive Health Care Advance Directive combines both the living will and the durable power of attorney for health care into one document, along with any other instructions you want followed, such as your desire to make an anatomical gift, as more fully discussed in Chapter 8 of this almanac.

AMENDMENT OR REVOCATION OF YOUR ADVANCE DIRECTIVE

Your advance directive continues to be in effect until and unless you revoke it. You are entitled to amend or revoke your advance directives at any time. If your advance directive is being amended, the changes should be made in writing, and signed, dated, and witnessed. Copies of the amended advance directive should be provided to all parties who received the original. If you are making substantial changes to your advance directives, it may be preferable to re-write the documents entirely. If you are revoking your advance directive, the revocation should also be made in writing, and signed, dated, and witnessed, with copies to all interested parties.

Nevertheless, whether or not you amended or revoked your advance directives, your physician must follow your oral statements regarding your health care decisions even if they contradict your written directives, provided you are able to communicate them directly to your physician.

MAKING SURE YOUR WISHES ARE CARRIED OUT

Most hospitals will allow you to keep a copy of your advance directives on file with them. Therefore, it is important to check with your hospital to make sure your advance directive documents conform to their requirements. If a hospital has a policy against advance directives, it is required to advise you at the time you are admitted.

You should also discuss your advance directives with your physician, particularly since a physician does not have the same obligation to inform you as a hospital does, therefore, you should inquire about any such policy up front.

If your physician or your hospital appears to be unwilling to comply with your wishes—e.g., on religious grounds—you should consider finding alternative medical care as soon as possible. In most states, a health care provider who refuses to honor a patient's health care advance directive is required to make reasonable efforts to transfer the patient to another health care provider who will comply.

Also discuss this matter with your family, so that they will be prepared if called on to support your decision. You must make your wishes known ahead of time to ensure that they will be followed.

You should keep the original health care directive in a place where it will easily be found in case you are unable to communicate. Copies should be given to your health care agent, your physician, designated hospitals or health care facilities, your minister or other religious advisor, certain family members, and your attorney. You may also carry a card with you, similar to an organ donor card, which contains basic information about the existence of your health care directives and contact information.

Your health care directive should be reviewed periodically, e.g., every five to ten years, depending on your age. You should also consider amending the document after certain events, such as marriage, divorce, retirement, diagnosis of illness, etc.

Some state statutes have made it a crime to falsify or forge a patient's advance health care directive, or to willfully conceal or withhold personal knowledge of the revocation of an advance directive. And, it is a felony if done with the intent to cause the withholding or withdrawal of life-sustaining treatment, or to artificially provide nutrition and hydration, contrary to the individual's wishes, and those actions hasten the patient's death.

MEDICAL BATTERY

A health care provider who imposes medical treatment contrary to the instructions left in an advance directive may be guilty of medical battery. Claims of battery against physicians for nonconsensual medical care have been recognized for some time even if the medical procedure is harmless, beneficial, or life-sustaining. The courts are becoming increasingly willing to find that battery has occurred in cases in which a health care provider refused to honor the directions left in an advance directive or given by an appointed agent.

CHAPTER 3:
THE LIVING WILL AND DURABLE POWER OF ATTORNEY FOR HEALTH CARE

WHAT IS A LIVING WILL?

A living will is a written declaration, directed to your physician, stating that you wish to forgo extraordinary treatment of a terminal illness, in order to die a natural death. A living will differs from an ordinary will in that a living will only specifies health care wishes whereas an ordinary will deals with the disposition of property upon your death.

Although living wills may not be statutorily recognized in all states, all 50 states and the District of Columbia have enacted laws providing for some type of living will, medical proxy, or health care durable power of attorney that governs the right of the patient, or the patient's designated representative, to make decisions about the patient's health care. Further, an individual has a constitutional right to execute a living will.

A sample Living Will is set forth at Appendix 5 of this almanac.

Purpose

The purpose of a living will is to give a person the right to decide the manner in which they will be treated should they develop an incurable illness or enter a persistent vegetative state, and become unable to communicate their wishes at that time. Generally, a living will provides that no heroic measures should be taken to prolong the individual's life where there is no reasonable expectation of recovery. However, pain medication is still usually administered.

A living will also provides family and loved ones some guidance in making a very painful decision. Further, a living will allows a health care provider to withdraw or withhold life-support treatment without risking a medical malpractice lawsuit.

Many state legislatures recognized the importance of the patient's right to make their own end-of-life health care decisions in enacting their living will statutes, as demonstrated by the legislative intent clause set forth in Alabama's *Natural Death Act:*

Natural Death Act [Code of Alabama §22-8A-2]

Legislative intent

The Legislature finds that competent adult persons have the right to control the decisions relating to the rendering of their own medical care, including, without limitation, the decision to have medical procedures, life-sustaining treatment, and artificially provided nutrition and hydration provided, withheld, or withdrawn in instances of terminal conditions and permanent unconsciousness.

In order that the rights of individuals may be respected even after they are no longer able to participate actively in decisions about themselves, the Legislature hereby declares that the laws of this state shall recognize the right of a competent adult person to make a written declaration instructing his or her physician to provide, withhold, or withdraw life-sustaining treatment and artificially provided nutrition and hydration or designate by lawful written form a health care proxy to make decisions on behalf of the adult person concerning the providing, withholding, or withdrawing of life-sustaining treatment and artificially provided nutrition and hydration in instances of terminal conditions and permanent unconsciousness. The Legislature further desires to provide for the appointment of surrogate decision-makers in instances where the individual has not made such a designation.

A table of state Living Will statutes is set forth at Appendix 6 of this almanac.

Requirements

There are certain requirements that must be met to ensure recognition of a living will.

Competency

Any adult over the age of 18 may execute a living will provided he or she is deemed to be competent, and acting of his or her own free will. If the individual is incapacitated at the time of the decision to provide, withhold, or withdraw life-sustaining treatment or artificially provided nutrition and hydration, a living will is generally presumed to be valid.

In the case of a minor, the minor's parents, or guardians appointed by the court, are generally relied upon by health-care providers as substitutes for the minor.

Diagnosis

In general, most states require that two physicians must diagnose the patient as terminally ill. Many states also provide that a living will is valid only if signed after the physician has informed the patient that he or she has an incurable illness. Before executing a living will, it is prudent to determine exactly what requirements are imposed in your state.

Form

A living will must be made in writing. There are many different living will forms available. There are official forms set forth in the state's living will statute, and unofficial forms created by state medical and bar associations, senior citizens' groups, and national right to die organizations, etc. Some states require the use of a statutory form for a living will to be valid.

Witnesses

A living will must be signed by the person executing the document—the "maker." Although state laws vary, living will statutes generally require that there be two witnesses to the maker's signature, neither of whom can be related to the maker or beneficiaries of his or her estate.

Medical Condition

A living will sets forth the medical condition under which the will would need to be consulted. A typical clause reads as follows:

MEDICAL CONDITION

1. If at any time I should have a terminal or incurable condition caused by injury, disease, or illness, certified to be terminal or incurable by at least two physicians, which within reasonable medical judgment would cause my death, and where the application of life-sustaining procedures would serve only to artificially prolong the moment of my death, I direct that such procedures be withheld or withdrawn, and that I be permitted to die with dignity.

2. If at any time I experience irreversible brain injury, or a disease, illness, or condition that results in my being in a permanent, irreversible vegetative or comatose state, and such injury, disease, illness, or condition would preclude any cognitive, meaningful, or functional future existence, I direct my physicians and any other attending nursing or

health care personnel to allow me to die with dignity, even if that requires the withdrawal or withholding of nutrition or hydration and my death will follow such withdrawal or withholding.

Life-Sustaining Treatment

A typical living will sets forth the type of life-sustaining treatment that may be provided, withheld or withdrawn. Basically, there are three general choices you can make regarding life-sustaining measures. You can request that:

1. Your health care providers do everything within their power to keep you alive;

2. The only life-sustaining measures you desire are nutrition (food) and hydration (water).

3. All artificial life-sustaining treatment is withheld, including nutrition and hydration.

Although it is not necessary to include every possible procedure to be provided, most living wills contain a clause setting forth the individual's intentions as to whether or not a certain "life-sustaining procedure" should be provided, withheld, or withdrawn if the individual's medical condition deteriorates. A typical clause reads as follows:

LIFE-SUSTAINING PROCEDURES

It is my expressed intent that the term "life-sustaining procedures" shall include not only medical or surgical procedures or interventions that utilize mechanical or other artificial means to sustain, restore, or supplant a vital function, but also shall include the placement, withdrawal, withholding, or maintenance of nasogastric tubes, gastrostomy, intravenous lines, heart-lung resuscitation, antibiotics, kidney dialysis, chemotherapy, or any other artificial, surgical, or invasive means for nutritional support and/or hydration.

Pain medication, nutrition and hydration are still usually given unless the living will specifically states that such treatment should be withheld.

Pregnancy Exclusions

Many living will statutes contain a pregnancy exclusion which provides that life-sustaining measures will continue regardless of any directive to the contrary until the pregnancy is complete, and that the pregnancy automatically invalidates the advance directive. For example, Missouri's law states:

"[T]he declaration to withdraw or withhold treatment by a patient diagnosed as pregnant by the attending physician shall have no effect during the course of the declarant's pregnancy." [Missouri Revised Statutes §49.025]

Other states use a viability standard to determine the enforceability of the advance directive. For example, Colorado's law states:

"In the case of a declaration of a qualified patient known to the attending physician to be pregnant, a medical evaluation shall be made as to whether the fetus is viable and could with a reasonable degree of medical certainty develop to live birth with continued application of life-sustaining procedures. If such is the case, the declaration shall be given no force or effect." [*Colorado Medical Treatment Decision Act* §15-18-104(2)].

A number of states are silent on the issue of pregnancy as it relates to a declaration contained in a living will. When a statute is silent, a court may be asked to decide whether the terms of the patient's living will would override the pregnancy. The court may hear testimony on this issue consisting of a patient's prior statements and conversations, to make its determination.

Amending or Revoking Your Living Will

As with any advance health care directive, you can amend your living will at any time, provided you are of sound mind and acting of your own free will. You may also revoke or terminate an existing living will without creating a new one. If you choose to amend your living will, and the changes you wish to make are minor, you should put the changes in writing, sign and date the amendment, and have it witnessed. Attached the amendment to your original living will and make sure all persons who received a copy also receive the amendment. If the changes you want to make are significant, it is advisable to start from the beginning and re-write your living will. Sign and date the new living will, have it witnessed, and provide a copy to everyone who was given copies of your prior living will.

DURABLE POWER OF ATTORNEY FOR HEALTH CARE

In order to have your wishes concerning medical treatment known and honored should you become incapacitated, you can designate a health care agent by executing what is generally known as a durable power of attorney for health care, also known as a "health care proxy" in some jurisdictions. In effect, the person you appoint "stands in your shoes" for the purposes of making your health care decisions.

Purpose

Both the living will and the durable power of attorney are types of advance directives, however, they serve two different purposes. The living will, which was developed before the durable power of attorney for health care, sets forth the patient's intentions in case of terminal illness or persistent unconsciousness. A durable power of attorney authorizes a health care agent to make health care decisions for the patient when he or she is no longer capable of making them.

A sample Durable Power of Attorney for Health Care is set forth in the Appendix 7 of this almanac.

Persons Authorized to Make Health Care Decisions

The individual is always the dominant source for health care decision-making. Even if another person assumes the decision-making role as agent, guardian, or surrogate, as set forth below, the decision-maker must always follow the individual's instructions.

Health Care Agent

As set forth above, an adult or emancipated minor may execute a durable power of attorney for health care and authorize a health care agent to make any health care decisions that he or she could have made while having capacity. Therefore, the appointment of a health care agent must be made very carefully.

In general, a designation of health care agent must be accepted in writing by the person designated to serve in that capacity. Therefore, it is important that you discuss your wishes thoroughly with the person you intend to appoint. You must make sure the person you appoint is comfortable with the directives contained in your living will, and is willing and able to carry out your wishes. The individual must be made aware that they could be called upon to discontinue life-sustaining procedures, and must be willing to take on this responsibility.

Alternate Health Care Agents

It is generally undesirable to appoint a "co-health care agent" as this can lead to disagreements and delays. However, you should designate one or two alternate health care agents. If your first choice for health care agent is not available, or unable to act when health care decisions must be made, the alternate health care agent is called upon to make your health care decisions. Otherwise, health care providers will make treatment decisions for you that follow instructions you gave while you were still able to do so. Any instructions that you write in your living will or durable power of attorney will guide health care providers under these circumstances.

Court-Appointed Guardian

If a guardian has been appointed by the court for the patient, the guardian may not revoke the health care agent's authority unless the court specifically authorizes a revocation. The health care agent's decision under an unrevoked power of attorney takes precedence over the guardian's decision. However, if there is no health care agent appointed, a guardian may make health-care decisions on behalf of the patient.

Surrogate

If the patient has not appointed a health care agent, and there is no court-appointed guardian, a surrogate may assume the authority to make health care decisions for the patient in the same manner as a health care agent under a durable power of attorney. A patient selects a surrogate by advising his or her health care provider of their choice for surrogate.

Relative

If a patient does not select a surrogate to make his or her health care decisions, then an individual related to the patient can step forward and assume the authority. Following is a list of family members, in priority order, who are generally authorized to make health care decisions of a patient if the patient did not select a health care agent or surrogate:

1. Spouse

2. Adult child

3. Parent

4. Adult brother or sister

If there is no available relative, the authority to make health care decisions for the patient may be assumed by an adult who has exhibited special care and concern for the patient, who is familiar with the patient's personal values, and who is willing and able to make a health care decision for the patient.

If the health care provider is unable to find any person who can qualify as a surrogate, the health care provider may ask a court to appoint a surrogate to make health care decisions for the patient.

Exclusions

Most states exclude the following people from appointment as a patient's health care agent:

1. The patient's doctor or other treating health care provider;

2. A non-relative employee of the patient's hospital or health care provider;

3. An operator of the patient's nursing home or assisted living facility;

4. A non-relative employee of the patient's nursing home or assisted living facility.

In addition, in some states, the divorce, dissolution, or annulment of the patient's marriage revokes the designation of the patient's former spouse as health care agent. If, following divorce, dissolution or annulment of the patient's marriage, the patient still desires a former spouse to act as their health care agent, they must state their choice in their health care agent designation, or in their order of divorce, dissolution, or annulment of marriage.

Treatment Decisions

The health care agent must make decisions regarding the providing, withholding, or withdrawing of life-sustaining treatment or artificially provided nutrition and hydration according to the patient's specific instructions contained in the patient's living will, if one was executed, or other instructions.

If there are no specific directions concerning a certain course of treatment, the health care agent's decisions must conform as closely as possible to what the patient would have wanted under the circumstances. The health care agent must take into account the patient's personal beliefs, moral values, religious view, etc. In addition, the health care agent must make a "burdens and benefits" analysis, as discussed in Chapter 1 of this almanac.

The health care agent exercises a lot of control over your health care and possible outcome if you become incapacitated. Thus, in writing your durable power of attorney, you must consider the scope of your health care agent's authority. You can limit your health care agent's authority, or you can give your health care agent very broad authority.

In general, you can give your health care agent the authority to:

1. Consent to, or refuse, medical treatment and procedures;

2. Employ or dismiss your health care providers;

3. Choose your health care facility;

4. Access your medical records;

5. Consent to pain and comfort medication;

6. Withhold hydration and nutrition; and

7. Take any other steps necessary to carry out your health care instructions.

However, unless your living will specifically provides that nutrition and hydration may be withdrawn or withheld, the health care agent is generally not permitted to make this decision.

Combining Your Living Will With a Health Care Proxy

Most states allow for a living will and a durable power of attorney to be combined into one document. However, if you execute both a living will and a durable power of attorney for health care, you must make sure that the terms of both documents are consistent to avoid confusion or invalidation. Discuss this matter with your physician and provide your physician with a copy of your documents.

A sample Living Will with Health Care Proxy is set forth at Appendix 8 of this almanac.

CHAPTER 4:
LANDMARK RIGHT-TO-DIE CASES

IN GENERAL

As the debate over the right to die continues, certain cases have received a lot of media attention. The three landmark cases discussed below have raised the awareness of both the public and the state legislatures about issues surrounding end-of-life health care decisions, such as the need for advance health care directives to avoid lengthy and emotionally devastating court battles.

THE KAREN ANN QUINLAN CASE

On April 15, 1975, Karen Ann Quinlan, age 21, attended a party where she ingested sedatives and alcohol. She went into cardiopulmonary arrest and became unconscious. Eventually, Karen fell into a persistent vegetative state. Karen did not have a living will or any other type of advance health care directive.

Karen's parents, the Quinlans, did not want to take any extraordinary means to keep Karen alive; however, the hospital officials disagreed and refused to disconnect Karen's respirator. The Quinlans believed that they had the right to make this decision as Karen's legal guardians. This led to two court battles over who should be Karen's legal guardian.

The Quinlans argued that, on at least three occasions, Karen had stated that she would not want to be kept alive if her medical condition was hopeless. However, the Superior Court of New Jersey found no evidence of Karen's prior statements. The state Attorney General, the hospital, Karen's treating physicians, and the county prosecutor, all argued that the state has an interest in preserving life, that there is no constitutional right to die, and that ceasing treatment would be homicide if Karen died. The Quinlans lost their first case at that level, and the Superior Court appointed a third party as Karen's legal guardian.

On March 31, 1976, almost one year after Karen fell into a coma, the Quinlans won on appeal to the New Jersey Supreme Court, and Karen's father was appointed her legal guardian. The New Jersey Supreme Court ruled that, despite her medical condition, Karen had a right to privacy, and the only way to permit Karen to exercise that right of privacy was to allow her family to render their best judgment concerning her medical condition. The Court established a "best interests" test whereby a surrogate is permitted to substitute their judgment in the best interests of an incapacitated patient when the wishes of the patient are unknown.

Regarding the state's interest in preserving life, the Court held that the state's interest weakens as the patient's prognosis worsens and the treatment becomes more invasive. The Court further held that disconnecting Karen's respirator is not homicide because withdrawing life-sustaining treatment does not cause death, but allows the disease to take its natural course, resulting in death.

In May 1976, Karen was weaned off of her respirator; however, she continued to breathe on her own. Karen's father did not want to stop artificial nutrition and hydration, even though the Supreme Court order permitted the withdrawal of all life-sustaining treatment. Karen Ann Quinlan died in 1985, 10 years after she lapsed into the coma.

The case of Karen Ann Quinlan established numerous precedents regarding an individual's right to die, and was largely responsible for the development and acceptance of advance health care directives. (In Re Quinlan, 70 N.J. 10, 355 A.2d 647 (1967)).

THE NANCY CRUZAN CASE

On December 11, 1983, Nancy Cruzan, age 25, was in a serious car accident. The police pronounced Nancy dead at the scene; however, paramedics were able to resuscitate her. Nancy was kept alive for years by artificial hydration and nutrition although she was diagnosed as being in a persistent vegetative state. Nancy did not have a living will or any other type of advance health care directive.

Nancy's parents, the Cruzans, eventually asked the health care facility to withhold the tube feedings so that Nancy could die a natural death, however, the facility refused to stop the feeding. The Cruzans were forced to go to court to obtain an order to stop the feedings. The trial court ruled that the feedings could be withheld, however, the health care facility appealed the ruling to the Missouri Supreme Court.

The Missouri Supreme Court reversed the trial court, stating that it required clear and convincing evidence that an incompetent patient would want to refuse treatment, such as a living will, thus severely restricting the family's right to make health care decisions. The case went to the U.S. Supreme Court.

In 1990, seven years after Nancy's accident, the U.S. Supreme Court upheld the Missouri Supreme Court's requirement that there be clear and convincing evidence of a person's expressed wishes made while they were still competent. After the U.S. Supreme Court ruling, the Cruzans petitioned the trial court in Missouri to rehear their request to discontinue Nancy's feedings. Based on testimony of new witnesses as to Nancy's wishes not to be kept alive by extraordinary means, authorization was given to stop the feedings, and Nancy Cruzan died shortly thereafter.

The case of Nancy Cruzan established the principle that competent adults have a constitutional right to refuse medical treatment, including the right to have life sustaining treatment withheld or withdrawn, but that a state may still require clear and convincing evidence of the patient's expressed wishes made while they were still competent. The Cruzan case furthered the development of advance health care directives, such as a living will and health care proxy. (Cruzan v. Director, 497 U.S. 261 (1990)).

THE TERRI SCHIAVO CASE

In February 1990, Terri Schiavo, age 27, was found unconscious on the bathroom floor by her husband. Terri had suffered a heart attack and severe loss of oxygen to her brain due to a potassium deficiency. She was subsequently diagnosed as being in a persistent vegetative state. Terri did not have a living will or any other type of advance health care directive.

In September 1993, acting as Terri's legal guardian, Michael Schiavo authorized the health care facility to issue a Do Not Resuscitate Order (DNR). He also refused to allow the facility to treat Terri with antibiotics for a potentially fatal infection, claiming that Terri's expressed wishes while competent were that she would not want to be kept alive in her medical condition. In response to this refusal of treatment, Terri's parents, the Schindlers, petitioned the court to have Terri's husband removed as guardian; however, Terri recovered from the infection and the guardianship petition was dismissed.

In 1997, Mr. Schiavo, through his lawyer, notified the Schindlers that he was going to authorize the withdrawal of artificial nutrition and hydration. The Schindlers again went to court to request an injunction to stop the withdrawal of Terri's feeding tube, arguing that they believed Terri's would have wanted treatment to continue despite what her husband's claims to the contrary.

In 2000, the court approved removal of Terri's feeding tube based on clear and convincing evidence that Terri would not have wanted life-sustaining treatment in her medical condition. The Schindlers filed an appeal to the Florida Appellate Court; however, the court upheld the lower court's decision to remove the feeding tube. The Florida Appellate Court issued a 30-day stay while the Schindlers appealed the decision to the Florida Supreme Court. The Florida Supreme Court upheld the two lower court decisions.

Following the Florida Supreme Court decision to permit the withdrawal of Terri's feeding tube, the Florida legislature enacted a law giving the governor the authority to override a court ruling in cases where a patient who has not executed a living will is in a persistent vegetative state, and family members cannot agree on the issue of life sustaining medical treatment.

In response, Mr. Schiavo filed suit challenging the constitutionality of the law. The trial court declared the statute unconstitutional, and the Florida Supreme Court upheld the lower court ruling on appeal. The U.S. Supreme Court refused to hear the case, thus, the ruling stood.

After all legislative and judicial attempts to keep Terri alive were exhausted, the feeding tube was finally removed and Terri Schiavo died on March 31, 2005, after having been in a persistent vegetative state for over 10 years. The Schiavo case captured the headlines and spawned a massive national and international debate over passive euthanasia, and generated increased interest in the topic of living wills. (In re Guardianship of Schiavo, 851 So. 2d 182, 183 (Fla. 2d DCA 2003)).

CHAPTER 5:
THE PATIENT SELF-DETERMINATION ACT

IN GENERAL

The *Patient Self-Determination Act* (PSDA) is a federal law that was passed by the U.S. Congress in 1990 and went into effect on December 1, 1991. The PSDA does not afford patients any new rights. It is the requirement that health care facilities advise patients of their already existing rights that makes this law so important.

Prior to enactment of the PSDA, many patients were unaware of their right to receive information that would help them make important decisions concerning their health care. Every individual has certain constitutionally protected rights regarding health care, such as the right to consent to, or refuse, treatment.

The intent of the PSDA is to make sure patients are able to protect these rights in case they become at some point unable to do so, thus allowing the individual to maintain control of his or her own health care choices to the greatest extent possible.

COVERED INSTITUTIONS

The PSDA governs virtually all health care facilities that receive Medicare or Medicaid funding, including hospitals, skilled nursing facilities, extended care facilities, hospice programs, health maintenance organizations, and home health care agencies. The only facilities that are exempt from the law are those institutions where the patients pay for their own health care services without any government assistance. This ensures that most individuals who receive health care will be covered by the law.

REQUIREMENTS OF THE PSDA

There are three important provisions of the PSDA detailing the obligations of: (1) covered health care facilities; (2) the individual states; and (3) the Secretary of the Department of Health and Human Services, as set forth below.

Obligations of Health Care Facilities

The PSDA is based on the concept of informed consent. Under the PSDA, covered health care facilities are required to give their patients information on applicable state laws regarding advance health care directives. As further discussed in Chapter 1, an advance directive refers to a written instruction executed by an individual which relates to the provision of health care should that individual become incapacitated, such as a living will or durable power of attorney for health care.

To comply with the PSDA requirements, patients must be given written information, upon admission to the facility, explaining their right to execute advance directives concerning their end-of-life care, and their right to participate in the decisions affecting their health care, including the following:

1. The patient's right to accept or refuse treatment;

2. The patient's rights under existing state laws, whether statutory or judge-made, regarding their right to formalize advance directives; and

3. Information concerning any written policies that the institution has concerning the implementation of the patient's rights.

The health care facility is also required to document each patient's medical record concerning the existence of any advance directives executed by the patient. Nevertheless, health care providers are expressly prohibited from conditioning the provision of care, or from otherwise discriminating against the patient, based on whether or not the individual has executed an advance directive.

In addition to the requirement to provide information to the patient, covered health care facilities must engage in ongoing educational activities for both their staff and the community on issues concerning advance directives, including the right to accept or refuse treatment and the opportunity for drafting or signing advance directives.

The PSDA also sets forth the time at which the patient is to receive the advance directives information, depending on the type of covered health care facility, as follows:

1. A hospital is required to provide the patient with this information at the time he or she is admitted as an inpatient.

2. A skilled nursing facility is required to provide the patient with this information at the time he or she is admitted as a resident.

3. Home health agencies are required to provide the patient with this information prior to the time the individual comes under the care of the agency.

4. Hospice programs are required to provide the patient with this information at the time hospice care is initiated.

5. Health maintenance organizations are required to provide the patient with this information at the time he or she enrolls in the plan.

In addition, the advance directives information must be provided to the patient each time he or she is admitted and/or comes under the care of a particular facility. For example, if an individual is first admitted to a hospital and then later transferred to a nursing home, both the hospital and the nursing home are required to independently provide the advance directives information to the individual upon admission.

Obligation of the Individual States

The PSDA requires each individual state to develop a written description of its law, whether statutory or judge-made, concerning the advanced directives that would be distributed by covered health care facilities.

Obligations of the Secretary of the Department of Health and Human Services

The PSDA requires the Secretary of the Department of Health and Human Services to:

1. Develop and implement a national campaign to inform the public of the option to execute advance directives, and of a patient's right to participate in, and control, his or her own health care decisions; and

2. Develop or approve nationwide information materials, to be distributed by health care providers, which would:

(a) inform the public and the medical and legal profession of the individual's right to make decisions concerning their medical care, including the right to accept or refuse treatment; and

(b) inform the public and the medical and legal profession of the existence of advance directives.

In addition, the Secretary is required to work with the individual states in preparing material concerning applicable state laws on the subject, to mail such information to all recipients of social security, and to include information concerning the PSDA in the Medicare handbook.

The *Patient Self-Determination Act* is set forth at Appendix 9 of this almanac.

CHAPTER 6:
THE UNIFORM HEALTH CARE DECISIONS ACT

IN GENERAL

In 1982, the National Conference of Commissioners on Uniform State Laws (NCCUSL) promulgated the Model Health-Care Consent Act, which addressed the broad issues of consent to treatment, but the Act did not address end-of-life decisions for terminal patients. The NCCUSL subsequently drafted the *Uniform Rights of the Terminally Ill Act* in 1985, amended in 1989, to address the narrower issues of dying patients.

Since that time, every state has enacted the use of some sort of advance health care directive, and most states have statutorily authorized the living will and the durable power of attorney for health care. However, there still exists inconsistency among state laws, which leads to conflict when an advance directive executed in one state must be implemented in another state.

Recognizing this problem, and the need for uniformity among state laws, in 1993, the NCCUSL drafted the *Health Care Decisions Act*. The Act is comprehensive and is designed to replace existing legislation concerning advance directives—e.g., living will, power of attorney and family consent statutes, etc.—with one all-encompassing statute. The Act has since been adopted by Alabama, Alaska, Delaware, Hawaii, Maine, Mississippi, New Mexico, and Wyoming.

PROVISIONS OF *THE HEALTH CARE DECISIONS ACT*

Patient's Rights

The Act acknowledges the right of a competent individual to decide all aspects of his or her own health care in all circumstances, including the right to refuse health care, or to withhold or withdraw treatment, even if it results in the patient's death. The Act also recognizes the individual's right to appoint a health care agent to carry out his or her wishes if the patient is incapacitated and unable to communicate his or her wishes.

Authorization of Health Care Decision Makers

The Act authorizes designated health care agents to make health care decisions for a patient who cannot or does not wish to make such decisions. The Act also authorizes a designated surrogate, family member, or close friend to make such decisions when a guardian or health care agent has not been appointed or is not available to serve in that capacity. If there is no person appointed or available to make health care decisions, the Act authorizes such decisions to be made by the appropriate court.

Form of Advance Directives

The Act simplifies and facilitates the drafting of advance health care directives. Under the Act, a health care instruction may be given orally or in writing. Further, a durable power of attorney for health care need not be witnessed or acknowledged, although the document must be in writing. The Act also sets forth a form of advance health care directive, the use of which is optional.

Patient's Instructions

The goal of the Act is to make sure that the patient's wishes concerning his or her health care are carried out. If the patient is incapacitated or otherwise unable to express those wishes, an authorized agent must make health care decisions in accordance with the patient's instructions to the extent known or, if unknown, in accordance with the best interests of the patient.

Compliance Requirements

The Act requires health care providers and institutions to comply with the patient's instructions, however, a health care provider or institution may decline to honor an instruction or decision for reasons of conscience or if the instruction or decision requires the provision of medically ineffective care or care contrary to applicable health-care standards. Nevertheless, the health care provider or institution must make a reasonable effort to transfer the patient to the care of a provider who will comply.

Under the Act, when a health care provider complies with the Act in good faith, the health care provider has immunity from prosecution and/or civil liability, even if the provider withdraws treatment that prolongs life.

Validity of Out-of-State Advance Health Care Directives

An important provision of the Act is that it ensures the validity of an advance health care directive regardless of when or where executed or communicated, thus an advance directive drafted in one state will be valid in any state that has adopted the Act.

Dispute Resolution

The Act sets forth a dispute resolution procedure and also authorizes a court to either enjoin or order a health care decision.

The *Uniform Health Care Decisions Act* is set forth at Appendix 10.

CHAPTER 7:
PHYSICIAN-ASSISTED SUICIDE

ASSISTED SUICIDE

Assisted suicide refers to the ending of one's life with the help of another. Unlike an advance health care directive, which is passive in nature, assisted suicide actively hastens death. Assisted suicide has also been referred to as mercy killing or active euthanasia. Although society at one time shunned the concept of assisted suicide and likened it to murder, the development of the law in this area seems to show that assisted suicide is gaining acceptance.

EUTHANASIA

Euthanasia, translated literally, simply means a "good death." The term has traditionally been used to refer to the hastening of a suffering person's death or "mercy killing," and it may be voluntary or involuntary. Involuntary active euthanasia is one of the least accepted social policies. It refers to an intervention that ends a patient's life without obtaining the informed consent of the patient. Voluntary active euthanasia involves an intervention requested by a competent individual that is administered to cause death, such as a lethal dose injection.

PHYSICIAN-ASSISTED SUICIDE DISTINGUISHED

Physician-assisted suicide is not the same as voluntary active euthanasia, although the outcome is the same. Physician-assisted suicide means the physician provides the patient with the means for death—usually a prescription for a lethal dose of medication.

It is the patient who administers the lethal medication, not the physician. Euthanasia means that the physician actively intervenes to end the patient's life, e.g., by administering a lethal injection.

As further discussed below, Oregon became the first state to permit physician-assisted suicide in limited circumstances when it enacted the Oregon *Death With Dignity Act* in 1994. Following passage of the Act, the Oregon Catholic Conference attempted to have it repealed. When that failed, they succeeded in bringing it up for a second vote that was held on November 4, 1997. The Act again passed with a resounding 60-40% victory, demonstrating the overwhelming support of the people for this right. A number of states have proposed similar legislation.

Proponents and opponents of physician-assisted suicide argue about whether the practice is ethical. Proponents argue that it is ethical because the physician is alleviating the suffering of a person who chooses to die rather than suffer without hope of recovery. Physician-assisted suicide is viewed as an individual's right to control over their end-of-life health care decisions, not unlike an advance health care directive.

Opponents argue that physician-assisted suicide is unethical because the physician's duty is to preserve life, not end it. They also fear that the patient's "right-to-die" may eventually turn into a coercive "duty-to-die" targeted at the elderly or infirm, to avoid more costly palliative care.

HISTORICAL BACKGROUND OF THE RIGHT-TO-DIE MOVEMENT

Debates over the right to die have been going on since the early 20th century, and a number of books were written on the topic, generally promoting assisted death and euthanasia. Some publications even offered directions on how to commit suicide, such as *Let Me Die Before I Wake*, published by the Hemlock Society in 1981.

Organizations

During the 1900s, many organizations were founded to support the concept of euthanasia, the first of which was the Euthanasia Society of America in 1938. In 1974, the Euthanasia Society of New York was renamed the Society for the Right to Die. In 1980, the Hemlock Society was founded in California as an advocate for right-to-die legislation. It was followed in 1986 by another California organization, Americans Against Human Suffering, which campaigned for passage of the 1992 *California Death with Dignity Act*, legislation that ultimately failed, as discussed below.

In 1991, two right-to-die organizations—Concern for Dying and Society for the Right to Die—merged, forming Choice in Dying, which became a strong advocate for living wills and patients' rights. In 1993, Compassion in Dying, a Washington organization, was formed to counsel terminally ill patients on assisted suicide, and challenge state laws prohibiting assisted suicide. In 2004, the Hemlock Society USA was re-named End-of-Life Choices and subsequently merged with Compassion in Dying to form a new organization, Compassion & Choices.

Physician-Assisted Suicide and the Law

Attempts to change the laws that ban physician-assisted suicide have generally been unsuccessful. Oregon is the only state that has been successful in this effort.

Early Attempts

In 1906, Ohio drafted the first assisted suicide bill, however, the legislation did not pass. A 1967 Florida right-to-die bill similarly failed, after extensive discussion in the legislature, and a voluntary euthanasia bill could not get passed in Idaho in 1969.

Arizona

In 2006, two right-to-die bills were introduced to the Arizona state legislature. The first one is similar to the law in Oregon and is called the *Aid in Dying* (HB2313). The second bill seeks to allow terminally ill patients to control their own medication (HB2314).

California

In 1992, Americans for Death with Dignity (formerly Americans Against Human Suffering), were successful in placing the *California Death with Dignity Act* on the state ballot. The Act proposed to allow physicians to assist terminally ill patients by actively administering, or prescribing medication to patients for self-administration, however, the initiative failed.

New York

In 1994, in Quill v. Koppell (870 F. Supp. 78, 84 (S.D.N.Y.1994)), New York's law criminalizing assisted suicide was upheld. On appeal, in 1996, the Second Circuit Court of Appeals reversed the Quill finding, ruling that the statute violated the Equal Protection Clause because it was not rationally related to any legitimate state interest. The ruling affects laws in New York, Vermont and Connecticut, however, the court stayed enforcement of its ruling for 30 days pending an appeal to the U.S. Supreme Court. In 1996, the U.S. Supreme Court agreed to hear the case and, in 1997, the Court reversed the lower court and upheld the state statute barring assisted suicide.

Oregon

In 1990, the Hemlock Society in Oregon introduced the *Death With Dignity Act* to the Oregon legislature, but the bill was unable to get out of committee at that time. In 1994, the voters approved the Oregon

Death With Dignity Act ballot initiative; however, the U.S. District Court issued an injunction barring the state from putting the law into effect.

In 1995, the U.S. District Court ruled that Oregon's *Death with Dignity Act* was unconstitutional because it violated the Equal Protection clause of the Constitution. In 1997, a measure that would have repealed the Act was defeated, and the Act finally took effect on October 27, 1997 after all court challenges had been concluded.

In 2003, after 129 terminally ill patients took advantage of physician-assisted suicide, the U.S. Attorney General asked the 9th Circuit Court of Appeal to reverse the finding of a lower court upholding the Oregon *Death With Dignity Act*. The Attorney General argued that states do not have the power to control lethal drugs, thus, the Act contravened federal powers. In 2005, the U.S. Supreme Court decided to take the Attorney General's case against the Oregon *Death With Dignity* law.

In 2006, the U.S. Supreme Court voted 6-3 to uphold the Oregon law, ruling that the former Attorney General had overstepped his authority in seeking to punish doctors who prescribed drugs to help terminally ill patients end their lives.

The Oregon Death with Dignity Act is discussed more fully below.

Rhode Island

In 2006, the Rhode Island *Death with Dignity Act*, modeled after the Oregon law, was introduced, however, the bill failed to emerge from committee before the legislative session ended.

Washington

In 1991, Washington voters rejected a physician-assisted suicide initiative. In 1994, Washington's anti-suicide law was overturned by a district court, which found that the law violated the 14th Amendment, however, the Ninth Circuit Court of Appeals reversed the decision on appeal, and reinstated the anti-suicide law.

In 1996, the Court reversed the finding and found that the ban on assisted suicide as it applied to competent, terminally ill adults violated the Due Process clause of the Constitution. However, in 1997, the Court reversed the lower court and upheld the state statute barring assisted suicide.

In 2006, the *Washington Death with Dignity Act* (SB6843) was introduced, however, this bill also failed to emerge from committee before the legislative session ended.

The Criminal Prosecution of Dr. Jack Kevorkian

In 1989, Dr. Jack Kevorkian, a pathologist, invented a "suicide machine" made out of parts from household tools and toy parts. He called the machine the "Thanatron" which translates to "death machine" in Greek. The intravenous machine was designed so that a terminally ill patient could press a button that would initially release a saline solution drip, then it would release a drug that would place the patient into a deep coma, and finally the machine would release a lethal dose of potassium chloride that stopped the patient's heart while they were asleep. Dr. Kevorkian referred to the suicide machine as a "dignified, humane and painless" way for a terminally ill patient to die whenever they wanted.

In 1990, Dr. Jack Kevorkian began defying a Michigan state law banning physician-assisted suicide by using his "suicide machine" to enable his first patient, Ms. Janet Adkins, to end her life. He was subsequently enjoined from assisting in any more suicides, but murder charges were dismissed in Ms. Adkins' death in 1990.

Dr. Kevorkian continued to assist in numerous patient suicides by various means. Michigan prosecutors attempted to bring charges against the doctor; however, their charges were routinely dismissed, as Michigan's law was unclear as to the legality of his actions.

In 1994, Michigan's ban on assisted suicide was upheld. In 1996, a Michigan jury acquitted Dr. Kevorkian of violating the law in two physician-assisted deaths. Thereafter, Dr. Kevorkian continued to engage in assisted suicides and, in September 1998, after assisting in his 92nd suicide in eight years, Michigan passed a law making assisted suicide a crime.

Nevertheless, Dr. Kevorkian continued to perform assisted suicides and, by November 1998, he had performed 120 procedures. After four failed criminal prosecutions, Dr. Kevorkian was finally convicted in 1999 and sentenced to 10-25 years in jail for the 2nd degree murder of Thomas Youk, after a video of his death by lethal injection was televised nationally. Meanwhile, a measure to legalize physician-assisted suicide in Michigan was defeated in 1998 by a vote of 70-30%.

THE OREGON DEATH WITH DIGNITY ACT

In 1997, Oregon enacted the *Death with Dignity Act* which allows physicians to provide a terminally ill patient with a prescription for a lethal dose of medication. As discussed above, the Act was a citizens' initiative passed twice by Oregon voters. The first time was in a general election in November 1994 when it passed by a margin of 51% to 49%. Nevertheless, the Act faced a lot of opposition.

An injunction delayed implementation of the Act until the injunction was lifted on October 27, 1997. In November 1997, a measure was placed on the general election ballot to repeal the *Death with Dignity Act*. Voters chose to retain the Act by a margin of 60% to 40%. In 2003, the U.S. Attorney General attempted to have the Act repealed, however, the U.S. Supreme Court voted 6-3 to uphold the law.

Oregon is the first state that has been able to enact a physician-assisted suicide law that has had the support of its voters and has been upheld by the U.S. Supreme Court. Many states seeking to enact similar laws have modeled their proposed legislation after the Oregon law.

The text of the Oregon *Death with Dignity Act* is set forth at Appendix 11 of this almanac.

Qualified Patient

Under the Act, it is the responsibility of "qualified" patients and licensed physicians to implement the Act on an individual basis. To be qualified, a patient must be:

1. 18 years of age or older;

2. A resident of Oregon;

3. Capable of making and communicating their own health care decisions, thus, family members cannot request the procedure on the patient's behalf, e.g., if the patient is in a coma; and

4. Diagnosed with a terminal illness that will lead to death within six (6) months.

The goal is to make sure that every patient who participates in the Act are doing so voluntarily, fully informed, and with the ability to make rational health care decisions for themselves. It is up to the attending physician to determine whether these criteria have been met.

Establishing Residency

In order to demonstrate residency, the patient must provide adequate documentation to the attending physician to verify that he or she is a current resident of Oregon. Adequate documentation includes but is not limited to:

1. A valid Oregon driver's license;

2. A lease demonstrating that the patient rents property in Oregon;

3. A deed or other ownership document demonstrating that the patient owns property in Oregon;

4. An Oregon voter registration card; or

5. A recent Oregon tax return.

There is no minimum residency requirement, and there is nothing in the law that prevents a non-resident from moving to Oregon to be covered by the Act. It is up to the attending physician to determine whether or not the patient has adequately established residency.

Qualified Physician

Patients who meet the above criteria can request a prescription for lethal medication from a licensed Oregon physician. The physician must be a Doctor of Medicine (M.D.) or Doctor of Osteopathy (D.O.) who is licensed to practice medicine by the Board of Medical Examiners for the State of Oregon.

Participation is voluntary, thus, physicians are not required to provide prescriptions to patients. If the attending physician does not participate in the program, the patient must find another qualified physician who is willing to participate. Out-of-state physicians cannot write the prescription.

Procedure for Obtaining Prescription

After it has been established that the patient has met the required criteria, and the doctor participates in the Act, the following steps must be taken in order to obtain the prescription:

1. The patient must make two oral requests to the attending physician for the prescription, separated by at least 15 days.

2. The patient must provide a written request for the prescription to the attending physician. The form is called a "Request for Medication to End My Life in a Humane and Dignified Manner." The request must be signed in the presence of two witnesses, at least one of whom is not related to the patient.

A copy of the Patient Request for Medication is set forth at Appendix 12 of this almanac.

3. The attending physician and a consulting physician must confirm the patient's diagnosis and prognosis.

4. The attending physician and a consulting physician must determine whether the patient is capable of making and communicating their own health care decisions.

5. If either physician believes the patient's judgment is impaired by a psychiatric or psychological disorder—e.g., depression—the patient must be referred for a psychological examination.

6. The attending physician must inform the patient of feasible alternatives, including comfort care, hospice care, and pain control.

7. The attending physician must request, but may not require, the patient to notify their next-of-kin of the prescription request.

A patient can rescind a prescription request at any time and in any manner. The attending physician will also offer the patient an opportunity to rescind his or her prescription request at the end of the 15-day waiting period following the initial request to participate.

It is up to the attending physician to make sure the patient meets all of the criteria under the Act. The physician must complete a compliance form verifying that all of the steps have been taken, and submit the form to the Oregon Department of Health Services.

A copy of the Attending Physician's Compliance Form is set forth at Appendix 13 of this almanac.

After all of the steps have been taken, it is up to the physician to determine the prescription drug to be taken. Most patients have received a prescription for a lethal oral dosage of a barbiturate. The law does not require the presence of the physician when the patient takes the lethal dose of medication, however, the physician may be present if the patient wishes, provided the physician does not administer the medication him/herself.

Insurance Concerns

Concerning health insurance coverage, individual insurance companies must determine whether the procedure is covered under their policies, just as they do with any other medical procedure. Nevertheless, federal funding cannot be used for services rendered under Oregon's Death with Dignity Act. For instance, the Oregon Medicaid program, which is paid for by federal funding, ensures that charges for services under the Act are paid only with state funds.

Concerning life insurance benefits, the Oregon statute specifies that participation under the Oregon *Death with Dignity Act* is not suicide, so it should not affect insurance benefits by that definition.

Euthanasia Distinguished

The Oregon *Death with Dignity Act* should not be confused with euthanasia. Euthanasia is illegal in every state, including Oregon. Euthanasia involves a legal injection of a lethal dose of medication by a physician. Under the *Death with Dignity Act*, a physician prescribes a lethal dose of medication to a patient, but the patient—not the physician—administers the medication.

CHAPTER 8:
ANATOMICAL DONATIONS

IN GENERAL

The rapid advancement of medical science since 1950, particularly in the area of organ transplantation, has given rise to an urgent need for organ donations. The number of people requiring a life-saving transplant continues to rise faster than the number of available donors.

From January through July 2006, 17,169 transplants were performed, and there were 8,671 donations. The gap between the donors and candidates continues to increase. As of October 2006, there were 93,581 waiting list candidates. Approximately 300 new transplant candidates are added to the waiting list each month, as advances in clinical medicine have allowed transplantation to become a treatment for their once hopeless diseases.

Numerous state statutes have been enacted during the past four decades to deal with the legal issues accompanying organ donation. Today, the concept of organ donation has become quite common, and all of the states have adopted the Uniform Anatomical Gift Act, which is discussed more fully below.

HOW TO BECOME AN ORGAN DONOR

The organ donor card was created to permit an individual to indicate the desire to donate organs. In many states, organ donor information is set forth on an individual's drivers license. You may also wish to indicate your desire to make an organ or body donation by placing a "statement regarding anatomical gifts" in your advance directives or will. The law provides that any provision in a will that concerns organ or body donations is not subject to probate, and will be considered valid, even if the will is ultimately declared invalid, as long as the gift was made in good faith.

A sample Statement Regarding Anatomical Gifts is set forth at Appendix 14 of this almanac.

Nevertheless, considering the limited time element for the usefulness of an anatomical gift, however, it is prudent to complete an organ donor card, which you can obtain from a local or national organ bank.

The language necessary to create a valid organ donation is quite simple. Basically, the following statement is all that is needed:

1. I wish to donate my organs and tissues.

2. I wish to give:

   (a) any needed organs and tissues;

   (b) only the following organs and tissues: [specify]

You should sign the card and have two witnesses also sign the card.

A sample Organ Donor Card is set forth at Appendix 15.

It is important to discuss your decision to be a donor with your family members and loved ones. Depending on the state, even if you sign a donor card, your family may be asked to sign a consent form in order for your donation to occur.

TYPES OF ANATOMICAL DONATIONS

Many types of organs, bones, and tissues are being transplanted today. Although heart and kidney transplants are probably the most common, there have also been medical breakthroughs permitting the transplantation of many additional body parts. Anatomical donations may include:

Blood Vessels

Blood vessels are the arteries, veins and capillaries through which blood circulates. Blood vessels can be donated and transplanted.

Bone

Bone is the dense tissue that forms the skeleton. Bone can be donated and transplanted, and is the most frequently used tissue. Bone plays an important role in curing birth and other defects and for back and dental surgery.

Bone Marrow

Bone marrow is the soft tissue located in the cavities of bones. Bone marrow is the source of all blood cells. Bone marrow can be donated and transplanted.

Eyes

Eye donations are commonly used in corneal transplants for corneal blindness, which accounts for approximately 20 percent of all blindness. The cornea, similar to a contact lens, is the transplant tissue that covers the iris, the colored part of the eye. A corneal transplant can give sight to a person suffering from corneal blindness. Corneal transplants must be performed shortly after the donor's death. Therefore, if you desire to make such a donation, it is advisable to complete a donor card in addition to including this provision in your advance directives and will. Eye donations are also used for research on the other causes of blindness.

Heart

The heart is a muscular organ that pumps blood through the body. Many types of fatal heart diseases can be treated successfully through transplantation.

Heart Valves

The heart valves consist of tissue that prevent the back flow of blood into the heart. The heart valves can be donated and transplanted.

Intestines

The intestines include that portion of the digestive track extending from the stomach to the anus, consisting of upper and lower segments. The intestines can be donated and transplanted.

Kidneys

The kidneys are a pair of organs that maintain proper water and electrolyte balance, regulate acid-base concentration, and filter the blood of metabolic waste, which is excreted as urine. There is an urgent need for kidneys to help the large number of persons presently suffering from kidney disease and failure. People on dialysis suffering from kidney disease may benefit from a transplant. A recipient of a kidney transplant will be given that chance to lead a more normal life.

Liver

The liver is a large reddish-brown organ that secretes bile and is active in the formation of certain blood proteins and in the metabolism of carbohydrates, fats, and proteins. Many children and adults suffering from severe liver disease will die without a liver transplant. Donations give them a second chance.

Lungs

The lungs are a pair of spongy organs that remove carbon dioxide from the blood and provide it with oxygen. Many types of fatal lung diseases can be treated successfully through transplantation.

Middle-Ear

The middle ear contains three small bones, in the shape of a hammer, anvil and stirrup. The ear is the organ of hearing and equilibrium. The middle-ear can be donated and transplanted.

Pancreas

The pancreas is a long, irregularly shaped gland, which lies behind the stomach, and secretes pancreatic juice into the lower end of the stomach. The pancreas aids in the digestion of proteins, carbohydrates, and fats. The pancreas can be donated and transplanted. Through pancreatic transplantation, diabetics no longer need daily insulin shots or face the possible loss of limbs, sight, or life.

Skin

Skin is the tissue forming the external covering of the body. A thin layer of skin—approximately 1/100th inch thick—may be donated and used as a temporary covering for burn wounds.

THE PROCESS OF DONATION

Organs are donated by individuals at the time of their death. The circumstances of the death and the health history of the donor determine which organs can be used. However, there are strict legal guidelines that must be followed before death can be certified and organs removed. These particular laws preclude a physician who has declared a person dead from being involved in the removal of that person's organs or the transplantation surgery itself.

BURIAL SERVICES FOR DONOR

Organ and tissue donation does not prevent family members from viewing the body or having a normal funeral service. Skilled medical personnel treat the body with the utmost respect and care. In the case of an organ donation, the deceased's body is normally returned, without the removed parts, to the person responsible for making the burial arrangements.

If you want to make sure that your body is preserved and your funeral and burial services are carried out according to your wishes, you should specify that request in your advance directives or will and expressly forbid those designated to carry out your request to make an anatomical donation upon your death.

In the case of a body donation, it is obviously impossible to provide for burial services at the time of death, but arrangements can be made for the return of the deceased's ashes to the family after cremation, upon release by the donee medical school.

THE COSTS OF DONATION

Since organ and tissue donation are gifts there is no cost to the family of the donor. By law, no payment can be made to them. All costs related to donation of organs and tissues are paid by the recipient, usually through insurance, Medicare or Medicaid. However, funeral expenses must still be paid by the donor's family.

THE ILLEGAL SALE OF HUMAN ORGANS AND TISSUES

The *National Organ Transplant Act* makes it illegal to sell human organs and tissues. Violators are subject to fines and imprisonment. Among the reasons for this rule is the concern of Congress that buying and selling of organs might lead to inequitable access to donor organs with the wealthy having an unfair advantage.

PERSONS AUTHORIZED TO MAKE ANATOMICAL GIFTS

All individuals of legal age can indicate their intent to donate their organs or tissue. In addition to the donor, the law also recognizes the authority of the deceased's relatives or other persons to authorize donations of the deceased's body or organs, unless the deceased has specifically forbidden such a gift. They are, in order of priority, the deceased's spouse, adult son or daughter, parent, adult sibling, guardian, or any other person who is authorized or obligated to dispose of the deceased's body.

Nevertheless, if the donation is opposed by anyone with equal status or priority over the person authorizing the donation, it cannot be made. Some states allow certain family members to veto an anatomical gift regardless of their priority status. Veto provisions vary among the states; therefore, the reader is advised to check the law of his or her jurisdiction in this regard.

There are no age limitations on who can donate. Newborns as well as senior citizens have been organ donors, however, individuals under 18 years of age must have their parent's or guardian's consent. The deciding factor on whether a person can donate is the person's physical condition, not the person's age. Regardless of any pre-existing medical circumstances or conditions, determination of suitability to donate organs or tissue may be based on a combination of factors that take into account the donor's general health and the urgency of need of the recipient.

Medical suitability for donation is determined at the time of death. This determination is usually done by the medical staff that recovers the organs or by the transplant team that reviews all of the data about the organs or tissue that have been recovered from the donor.

DONEES AUTHORIZED TO RECEIVE ANATOMICAL GIFTS

An anatomical donation does not have to name any particular donee. Those authorized by law to receive such donations include hospitals, surgeons, physicians, medical and dental schools, organ banks—e.g., eye banks, and specified individuals who require donations.

Individual donees are matched to organs based on a number of factors including blood and tissue typing, medical urgency, time on the waiting list, and geographical location. A specified donee may accept or reject the donation. If the specified donee rejects the donation or it is impossible to comply with the donor's wishes, another donee may accept the donation instead.

A person may also donate his or her body, or any of its parts, for the use of medical science. There is a great need by medical schools for body donations to ensure that physicians and surgeons receive the best possible training, including development of the ability and skill required to perform new and/or difficult surgical procedures. If you would like to donate your body to a medical school, you should contact the school of your choice and request further information on the procedure and any forms that they may require.

REVOCATION OF AN ANATOMICAL GIFT

If you change your mind at any time and choose not to make an anatomical donation, you should discard your organ donor card and cancel any other document you may have completed authorizing such a donation. In addition, if you made such a provision in your will, you should revoke the existing will and make an entirely new will.

THE UNIFORM ANATOMICAL GIFT ACT

The *Uniform Anatomical Gift Act* ("the Act") was promulgated by the National Conference of the Commissioners on Uniform State Laws, with the assistance of the medical profession, to provide guidelines for anatomical donations after death for the use of medical science. By 1972, the Act had been adopted by all 50 states.

Under the Act, any mentally competent adult can make a donation of his or her body or organs, which becomes effective upon death. In addition, certain authorized persons, usually family members, can authorize such donations according to the Act and pursuant to any additional provisions of the specific state statute.

The donor can specify the manner in which their anatomical donation is to be carried out and choose from a variety of alternatives. For example, the donor can donate all or certain parts of their body, and may set forth their wishes concerning funeral and burial services. The donation must, however, be used for purposes of transplantation, medical or dental research and education, or the advancement of medical or dental science.

APPENDIX 1:
THE AMA STATEMENT ON WITHHOLDING OR WITHDRAWING OF LIFE-PROLONGING MEDICAL TREATMENT

The social commitment of the physician is to sustain life and relieve suffering. Where the performance of one duty conflicts with the other, the choice of the patient, or his family or legal representative if the patient is incompetent to act in his own behalf, should prevail. In the absence of the patient's choice or an authorized proxy, the physician must act in the best interest of the patient.

For humane reasons, with informed consent, a physician may do what is medically necessary to alleviate severe pain, or cease or omit treatment to permit a terminally ill patient whose death is imminent to die. However, he should not intentionally cause death. In deciding whether the administration of potentially life-prolonging medical treatment is in the best interest of the patient who is incompetent to act in his own behalf, the physician should determine what the possibility is for extending life under humane and comfortable conditions and what are the prior expressed wishes of the patient and attitudes of the family or those who have responsibility for the custody of the patient.

Even if death is not imminent but a patient's coma is beyond doubt irreversible and there are adequate safeguards to confirm the accuracy of the diagnosis and with the concurrence of those who have responsibility for the care of the patient, it is not unethical to discontinue all means of life-prolonging medical treatment.

Life-prolonging medical treatment includes medication and artificially or technologically supplied respiration, nutrition or hydration. In treating a terminally ill or irreversibly comatose patient, the physician should determine whether the benefits of treatment outweigh its burdens. At all times, the dignity of the patient should be maintained.

APPENDIX 2:
SAMPLE DO NOT RESUSCITATE ORDER ("DNR ORDER")

Patient Name:

Patient Date of Birth:

DO NOT RESUSCITATE THE PERSON NAMED ABOVE. IF IN CARDIAC ARREST, THE INDIVIDUAL NAMED ABOVE IS TO RECEIVE NO CARDIOPULMONARY RESUSCITATION (CPR), NO ELECTRIC DEFIBRILLATION, NO TRACHEAL INTUBATION, AND NO VENTILATORY ASSISTANCE.

Effective Date:

Physician's Signature:

Print Physician's Name:

CONSENT

I understand that this document is a Do Not Resuscitate Order. I further understand that, in the event of suffering cardiac arrest, I am refusing cardiopulmonary resuscitation in situations where death may be imminent. I make this request knowingly and I am aware of the alternatives. I expressly release, on behalf of myself and my family, all persons who shall in the future attend to my medical care of any and all liability whatsoever for acting in accordance with this request.

Furthermore, I direct that these guidelines be enforced even though I may develop a diminished mental capacity in the future. I am aware that I may revoke these instructions at any time by:

(1) the physical destruction or verbal rescinding of this order by the physician who signed it; or

(2) by the physical destruction or verbal rescinding of this order by the person who gave written informed consent to the order, including

myself or my legally authorized guardian, agent, or surrogate decision maker.

[Authorized signature of patient or patient's health care agent, surrogate decision maker or legal guardian]

APPENDIX 3:
RELEASE FROM LIABILITY FOR DISCONTINUING LIFE-SUSTAINING PROCEDURES

[I/we], the undersigned, are the [guardian/family/health care agent] of [insert patient name]. (His/her) attending physician [name of physician] has advised that [insert patient name] has suffered severe and irreversible brain injury that precludes any cognitive, meaningful or functional future existence. [Note: Or set forth a similar statement of the patient's condition].

We understand that (his/her) current survival is contingent upon [insert the procedure to be withheld or withdrawn]. It is our desire and that of the patient as expressed in (his/her) Living Will, Health Care Declaration, Durable Power of Attorney, and/or Appointment of Health Care Agent, a copy of which is attached hereto, executed on [date[s]], that all "life-sustaining procedures" as therein defined be discontinued.

By (my/our) signature(s), (I/we) hereby release and agree to hold harmless (his/her) the physicians, nurses and staff of [name of facility], as well as [name of facility], from any liability, claims for damages, or causes of action that might otherwise be brought as a result of the death that likely will occur subsequent to the discontinuance of the above-described life-sustaining procedures.

SIGNATURE LINE/ADDRESS/DATE – RELEASOR [guardian/next of kin/health care agent]

RELATIONSHIP TO PATIENT: [specify relationship]

SIGNATURE LINE/ADDRESS/DATE – WITNESS #1

SIGNATURE LINE/ADDRESS/DATE – WITNESS #2

NOTARIAL ACKNOWLEDGMENT

BEFORE ME, the undersigned authority, on this day personally appeared [insert name of releasor], and [names of two witnesses], known to me to be the releasor and witnesses whose names are subscribed to the foregoing instrument in their respective capacities, and, all of said persons being by me duly sworn, [name of releasor] declared to me and to the said witnesses in my presence that said instrument is a release of liability, and that (he/she) had willingly and voluntarily made and executed it as (his/her) free act and deed for the purposes therein expressed.

SUBSCRIBED AND SWORN TO BEFORE ME by the releasor, [insert name] and by the witnesses [insert names] this _____ day of _____, 20_____.

_____
NOTARY PUBLIC

APPENDIX 4:
INFORMED CONSENT AGREEMENT

I, [insert patient name] allow [insert physician name] to perform upon me an operation known as [type of operation to be performed, e.g., appendectomy, mastectomy, etc.]. I further understand that my physician may be assisted in performing this operation by [list names of any assisting physicians, if applicable], but that the operation will be primarily performed by [name of physician].

I have been informed that [insert physician name] has performed [#] [type of operation[s]] during the last 12 months and that the mortality rate was [xx%], the infection rate was [xx%] and the mistake rate was [xx%].

The hospital, [insert hospital name], has informed me that [#] related operations were performed during the last 12 months at this facility and that the mortality rate was [xx%], the infection rate was [xx%], and the mistake rate was [xx%].

My physician, [insert physician name], and this hospital, [insert hospital name], carry liability insurance in the amount of [insert dollar amount] and [insert dollar amount] respectively. This liability insurance [is/is not] approximately the same as other physicians and hospitals performing this operation would be expected to carry to provide compensation to patients who may die or be injured by medical mismanagement.

I have been informed that a [type of operation] is a (major/minor) operation and will be performed as described below:

[Describe in detail the procedure to be performed as well as the physician's rights to perform further surgery if an unexpected condition is encountered during the course of the surgery].

As with any major surgery, bleeding can occur and at times can be serious. In addition, infection can occur and the risks of developing such an infection are as reported above.   [Describe all further risks of the procedure in detail].

I have been informed that the recovery period for this type of operation is as follows. [Describe details of recovery period].

I have been advised that a [type of operation] is necessary because [provide details as to why the particular procedure is necessary].

I have been advised that the alternatives of treatment include [provide details of all alternative treatments available, including the possible outcome and risks associated with the alternative treatments].

I have been advised that it is the opinion of my physician that a [type of operation] is indicated and the risks of the operation are less than the alternatives, and I have been given the opportunity of seeking independent consultation prior to having this surgery.

Although I have been fully informed about the risks of undergoing a [type of procedure], I am willing to undergo the operation. This does not relieve my physician of any responsibilities for acts of negligence, which would include rendering substandard care to me, causing injuries that should not have occurred, even though I am aware that there may be a risk in having the operation performed. I agree to undergo a [type of operation] after being fully informed, but expect that proper care shall be rendered to me at all times. This includes post-operative care by my physicians and the nurses and hospital personnel.

SIGNATURE LINE/DATE—PATIENT

SIGNATURE LINE/DATE—PHYSICIAN

APPENDIX 5:
LIVING WILL

DECLARATION made this [insert date].

I, [insert declarant's name and address], being of sound mind, willfully and voluntarily make known my desire that my life shall not be artificially prolonged under the circumstances set forth below, and do hereby declare:

MEDICAL CONDITION

1. If at any time I should have a terminal or incurable condition caused by injury, disease, or illness, certified to be terminal or incurable by at least two physicians, which within reasonable medical judgment would cause my death, and where the application of life-sustaining procedures would serve only to artificially prolong the moment of my death, I direct that such procedures be withheld or withdrawn, and that I be permitted to die with dignity.

2. If at any time I experience irreversible brain injury, or a disease, illness, or condition that results in my being in a permanent, irreversible vegetative or comatose state, and such injury, disease, illness, or condition would preclude any cognitive, meaningful, or functional future existence, I direct my physicians and any other attending nursing or health care personnel to allow me to die with dignity, even if that requires the withdrawal or withholding of nutrition or hydration and my death will follow such withdrawal or withholding.

LIFE-SUSTAINING PROCEDURES

It is my expressed intent that the term "life-sustaining procedures" shall include not only medical or surgical procedures or interventions that utilize mechanical or other artificial means to sustain, restore, or supplant a vital function, but also shall include the placement, withdrawal, withholding, or maintenance of nasogastric tubes, gastrostomy, intravenous lines, or any other artificial, surgical, or invasive means for nutritional support and/or hydration.

"Life-sustaining procedures" shall not be interpreted to include the administration of medication or the performance of any medical procedure deemed necessary to provide routine care and comfort or alleviate pain.

RIGHT TO REFUSE TREATMENT

It is my intent and expressed desire that this Declaration shall be honored by my family, physicians, nurses, and any other attending health care personnel as the final expression of my constitutional and legal right to refuse medical or surgical treatment and to accept the consequences of such refusal. Any ambiguities, questions, or uncertainties that might arise in the reading, interpretation, or implementation of this Declaration shall be resolved in a manner to give complete expression to my legal right to refuse treatment and shall be construed as clear and convincing evidence of my intentions and desires.

REVOCATION OF PREVIOUSLY EXECUTED DOCUMENTS

I understand the full importance of this Declaration and I am emotionally and mentally competent to make this Declaration, and by my execution, I hereby revoke any previously executed Health Care Declaration.

COPIES AND DISTRIBUTION

The original of this document is kept at [insert address where original document is kept]. I have made [#] copies of this document. Numbered and signed copies have been provided to the following individuals and/or institutions: [List names, addresses and phone numbers of individuals and/or institutions holding copies of the document].

Signed in the presence of the witnesses who have signed below this _____ day of _____, 20__.

SIGNATURE LINE – DECLARANT

STATEMENT OF WITNESSES

I state this [insert date], under penalty of perjury, that the Declarant has identified (himself/herself) to me and that the Declarant signed or acknowledged this Health Care Declaration in my presence.

I believe the Declarant to be of sound mind, and the Declarant has affirmed (his/her) awareness of the nature of this document and is signing it voluntarily and free from duress. The Declarant requested that I serve as a witness to (his/her) execution of this document.

I declare that I am not related to the Declarant by blood, marriage, or adoption and that to the best of my knowledge I am not entitled to any part of the estate of the Declarant on the death of the principal under a will or by operation of law.

I am not a provider of health or residential care, an employee of a provider of health or residential care, the operator of a community care facility, or an employee of an operator of a health care facility.

I declare that I have no claim against any portion of the estate of the Declarant upon (his/her) death, nor any personal financial responsibility for the payment of Declarant's medical bills or any other of Declarant's obligations.

SIGNATURE LINE/ADDRESS/DATE – WITNESS #1

SIGNATURE LINE/ADDRESS/DATE – WITNESS #2

SIGNATURE LINE/ADDRESS/DATE – WITNESS #3

NOTARIAL ACKNOWLEDGMENT

BEFORE ME, the undersigned authority, on this day personally appeared [insert name of declarant], and [names of three witnesses], known to me to be the declarant and witnesses whose names are subscribed to the foregoing instrument in their respective capacities, and, all of said persons being by me duly sworn, [name of declarant] declared to me and to the said witnesses in my presence that said instrument is (his/her) Living Will, and that (he/she) had willingly and voluntarily made and executed it as (his/her) free act and deed for the purposes therein expressed.

SUBSCRIBED AND SWORN TO BEFORE ME by the declarant, [insert name] and by the witnesses [insert names] this _____ day of _____, 20_____.

_____

NOTARY PUBLIC

APPENDIX 6:
TABLE OF STATE LIVING WILL STATUTES

STATE	STATUTE	SECTION
Alabama	Natural Death Act	Code of Alabama §22-8A-1 et seq.
Alaska	Rights of Terminally Ill Act	Alaska Statutes §18.12.010 et seq.
Arizona	Medical Treatment Decision Act	Arizona Revised Statutes §36-3201 et seq.
Arkansas	Rights of the Terminally Ill or Permanently Unconscious Act	Arkansas Statutes Annotated §20-17-202 et seq.
California	Health Care Decisions Law	California Probate Code §4670 et seq.
Colorado	Medical Treatment Decision Act	Colorado Revised Statutes §15-18-101 et seq.
Connecticut	Removal of Life Support Systems	Connecticut General Statutes Annotated §19a-570 et seq.
Delaware	Delaware Death with Dignity Act	Delaware Code Annotated Title 16 §2501 et seq.
District of Columbia	Natural Death Act	District of Columbia Code §7-621 et seq.
Florida	Life Prolonging Procedure Act	Florida Statutes Annotated §765.301 et seq.
Georgia	Living Wills Act	Code of Georgia §31-32-1 et seq.
Hawaii	Medical Treatment Decisions Act	Hawaii Revised Statutes §327E-1 et seq.
Idaho	Natural Death Act	Idaho Code §39-4501 et seq.
Illinois	Living Will Act	Illinois Revised Statutes Chapter 755 §35/1 et seq.
Indiana	Living Wills and Life Prolonging Procedures Act	Indiana Code Annotated §16-36-4-1 et seq.
Iowa	Life Sustaining Procedures Act	Code of Iowa §144A.3 et seq.
Kansas	Natural Death Act	Kansas Statutes Annotated §65-28.101 et seq.
Kentucky	Living Will Act	Kentucky Revised Statutes §311.621 et seq.

Louisiana	Natural Death Act	Louisiana Revised Statutes Title 40 §1299.58.1 et seq.
Maine	Living Will Act	Maine Revised Statutes Annotated Title 18-A §5-801 et seq.
Maryland	Life Sustaining Procedures Act	Maryland Health General Code Annotated Title 5 §5-601 et seq.
Massachusetts	N/A	No statutory provision for a living will
Michigan	N/A	No statutory provision for a living will
Minnesota	Adult Health Care Decisions Act	Minnesota Statutes §145B.01 et seq.
Mississippi	Natural Death Act	Mississippi Code Annotated §41-41-201 et seq.
Missouri	Life Support Declaration	Annotated Missouri Statutes §459.015 et seq.
Montana	Living Will Act	Revised Montana Code Annotated §50-9-101 et seq.
Nebraska	Rights of the Terminally Ill Act	§20-401 et seq.
Nevada	Living Will Statute	Nevada Revised Statutes §449.535 et seq.
New Hampshire	Terminal Care Document	New Hampshire Revised Statutes Annotated §137-H:1 et seq.
New Jersey	Living Will Statute	New Jersey Statutes Annotated §26:2H-53 et seq.
New Mexico	Right to Die Act	New Mexico Statutes Annotated §24-7A-1 et seq.
New York	Public Health Law	Article 29-B; 29-C §2964 et seq.
North Carolina	Natural Death Act	General Statutes of North Carolina §90-320 et seq.
North Dakota	Uniform Rights of Terminally Ill Act	North Dakota Century Code §23-06.4-01 et seq.
Ohio	Living Will Statute	Ohio Revised Code Annotated §2133.01 et seq.
Oklahoma	Natural Death Act	Oklahoma Statutes Annotated Title 63, Ch. 60, §3101.1 et seq.
Oregon	Directive to Physicians	Oregon Revised Statutes §127.505 et seq.
Pennsylvania	Advance Directive for Health Care	Pennsylvania Consolidated Statutes Chapter 54 Title 20 §5401 et seq.
Rhode Island	Rights of the Terminally Ill Act	§23-4.11-1 et seq.
South Carolina	Death with Dignity Act	Code of Laws of South Carolina §44-77-10 et seq.
South Dakota	Living Will Statute	South Dakota Codified Laws Annotated §34-12D-1 et seq.

Tennessee	Right to Natural Death Act	Tennessee Code Annotated §32-11-101 et seq.
Texas	Advance Directives	Texas Health and Safety Code §166.031 et seq.
Utah	Personal Choice and Living Will Act	Utah Code Annotated §75-2-1101 et seq.
Vermont	Terminal Care Document	Vermont Statutes Annotated Title 18, Chapter 111 §5251 et seq.
Virginia	Natural Death Act	Code of Virginia Annotated §54.1-2981 et seq.
Washington	Natural Death Act	Washington Revised Code Annotated §70-122.010 et seq.
West Virginia	Natural Death Act	West Virginia Code Article 30 §16-30-1 et seq.
Wisconsin	Natural Death Act	Wisconsin Statutes Annotated §154.01 et seq.
Wyoming	Living Will Act	Wyoming Statutes §35-22-101 et seq.

APPENDIX 7:
DURABLE POWER OF ATTORNEY FOR HEALTH CARE

APPOINTMENT made this [insert date].

I, [insert declarant's name and address], being of sound mind, willfully and voluntarily appoint [insert health care agent's name/address/telephone number], as my Health Care Agent (hereinafter "Agent") with a Durable Power of Attorney to make any and all health care decisions for me, except to the extent stated otherwise in this document.

EFFECTIVE DATE

This Durable Power of Attorney and Appointment of Health Care Agent shall take effect at such time as I become comatose, incapacitated, or otherwise mentally or physically incapable of giving directions or consent regarding the use of life-sustaining procedures or any other health care measures.

"Health care" in this context means any treatment, service, or procedure utilized to maintain, diagnose, or treat any physical or mental condition.

DETERMINATION OF MEDICAL CONDITION

A determination of incapacity shall be certified by my attending physician and by a second physician who is neither employed by the facility where I am a patient nor associated in practice with my attending physician and who shall be appointed to independently assess and evaluate my capacity by the appropriate administrator of the facility where I am a patient.

AUTHORITY OF HEALTH CARE AGENT

My health care agent is authorized, in consultation with my attending physician, to direct the withdrawal or withholding of any life-sustaining procedures, as defined herein, as (he/she) solely in the exercise of (his/her) judgment shall determine are appropriate to comply with my wishes and desires.

In addition, my Agent by acceptance of this Appointment agrees and is hereby directed to use (his/her) best efforts to make those decisions that I would make in the exercise of my right to refuse treatment and not those that (he/she) or others might believe to be in my best interests.

APPOINTMENT OF ALTERNATE AGENTS

If the person designated as my Agent is unable or unwilling to accept this Appointment, I designate the following persons to serve as my Agent to make health care decisions for me as authorized by this document. They shall serve in the following order:

1. First Alternate Agent: [insert name/address/telephone number]

2. Second Alternate Agent: [insert name/address/telephone number]

DURATION

[Option 1] I understand that this Power of Attorney exists indefinitely unless I define a shorter time herein or execute a revocation. If I am incapacitated at such time as this Power of Attorney expires (if applicable), the authority I have granted my Agent shall continue until such time as I am capable of giving directions regarding my health care.

[Option 2] This power of attorney ends on the following date: [insert termination date].

COPIES AND DISTRIBUTION

The original of this document is kept at [insert address where original document is kept]. I have made [#] copies of this document. Numbered and signed copies have been provided to the following individuals or institutions: [List names, addresses and phone numbers of individuals and/or institutions holding copies of the document].

Signed in the presence of the witnesses who have signed below this _____ day of _____, 20__.

SIGNATURE LINE – DECLARANT

STATEMENT OF WITNESSES

I state this [enter date], under penalty of perjury, that the Declarant has identified (himself/herself) to me and that the Declarant signed or acknowledged this Durable Power of Attorney and Appointment of Health Care Agent in my presence.

I believe the Declarant to be of sound mind, and the Declarant has affirmed (his/her) awareness of the nature of this document and is signing it voluntarily and free from duress. The Declarant requested that I serve as a witness to (his/her) execution of this document.

I declare that I am not related to the Declarant by blood, marriage, or adoption and that to the best of my knowledge I am not entitled to any part of the estate of the Declarant on the death of the principal under a will or by operation of law.

I am not a provider of health or residential care, an employee of a provider of health or residential care, the operator of a community care facility, or an employee of an operator of a health care facility.

I declare that I have no claim against any portion of the estate of the Declarant upon (his/her) death, nor any personal financial responsibility for the payment of Declarant's medical bills or any other of Declarant's obligations.

SIGNATURE LINE/ADDRESS/DATE – WITNESS #1

SIGNATURE LINE/ADDRESS/DATE – WITNESS #2

SIGNATURE LINE/ADDRESS/DATE – WITNESS #3

ACCEPTANCE BY HEALTH CARE AGENTS

HEALTH CARE AGENT (First Choice)

I, [insert name of health care agent], am willing to serve and accept the appointment as the health care agent for [insert name of declarant] as described in this document.

SIGNATURE LINE/ADDRESS/DATE – HEALTH CARE AGENT

HEALTH CARE AGENT (First Alternate)

I, [insert name of first alternate health care agent], am willing to serve and accept the appointment as the health care agent for [insert name of declarant] as described in this document, if the declarant's first choice cannot serve as health care agent.

SIGNATURE LINE/ADDRESS/DATE – HEALTH CARE AGENT (First Alternate)

HEALTH CARE AGENT (Second Alternate)

I, [insert name of second alternate health care agent], am willing to serve and accept the appointment as the health care agent for [insert name of declarant] as described in this document, if neither the declarant's first choice nor first alternate can serve as health care agent.

SIGNATURE LINE/ADDRESS/DATE – HEALTH CARE AGENT (Second Alternate)

NOTARIAL ACKNOWLEDGMENT

BEFORE ME, the undersigned authority, on this day personally appeared [insert name of declarant], and [names of three witnesses], and [names of three health care agents] known to me to be the declarant, witnesses, and health care agents whose names are subscribed to the foregoing instrument in their respective capacities, and, all of said persons being by me duly sworn, [name of declarant] declared to me and to the said witnesses in my presence that said instrument is (his/her) Durable Power of Attorney for Health Care, and that (he/she) had willingly and voluntarily made and executed it as (his/her) free act and deed for the purposes therein expressed.

SUBSCRIBED AND SWORN TO BEFORE ME by the declarant, [insert name], by the witnesses [insert names], and by the health care agents [insert names] this _____ day of _____,20_____.

_____

NOTARY PUBLIC

APPENDIX 8:
SAMPLE LIVING WILL WITH DURABLE
POWER OF ATTORNEY FOR HEALTH CARE

SECTION 1. LIVING WILL

I, [insert declarant's name and address], being of sound mind and at least 19 years old, would like to make the following wishes known. I direct that my family, my doctors and health care workers, and all others follow the directions I am writing down. I know that at any time I can change my mind about these directions by tearing up this form and writing a new one. I can also do away with these directions by tearing them up and by telling someone at least 19 years of age of my wishes and asking him or her to write them down.

I understand that these directions will only be used if I am not able to speak for myself.

IF I BECOME TERMINALLY ILL OR INJURED:

Terminally ill or injured is when my doctor and another doctor decide that I have a condition that cannot be cured and that I will likely die in the near future from this condition.

Life sustaining treatment—Life sustaining treatment includes drugs, machines, or medical procedures that would keep me alive but would not cure me. I know that even if I choose not to have life sustaining treatment, I will still get medicines and treatments that ease my pain and keep me comfortable.

PLACE YOUR INITIALS BY EITHER "YES" OR "NO":

I want to have life sustaining treatment if I am terminally ill or injured. ____ Yes ____ No

Artificially provided food and hydration (Food and water through a tube or an IV)—I understand that if I am terminally ill or injured I may need to be given food and water through a tube or an IV to keep me alive if I can no longer chew or swallow on my own or with someone helping me.

PLACE YOUR INITIALS BY EITHER "YES" OR "NO":

I want to have food and water provided through a tube or an IV if I am terminally ill or injured. ____ Yes ____ No

IF I BECOME PERMANENTLY UNCONSCIOUS:

Permanent unconsciousness is when my doctor and another doctor agree that within a reasonable degree of medical certainty I can no longer think, feel anything, knowingly move, or be aware of being alive. They believe this condition will last indefinitely without hope for improvement and have watched me long enough to make that decision. I understand that at least one of these doctors must be qualified to make such a diagnosis.

Life sustaining treatment—Life sustaining treatment includes drugs, machines, or other medical procedures that would keep me alive but would not cure me. I know that even if I choose not to have life sustaining treatment, I will still get medicines and treatments that ease my pain and keep me comfortable.

PLACE YOUR INITIALS BY EITHER "YES" OR "NO":

I want to have life-sustaining treatment if I am permanently unconscious. ____ Yes ____ No

Artificially provided food and hydration (Food and water through a tube or an IV)—I understand that if I become permanently unconscious, I may need to be given food and water through a tube or an IV to keep me alive if I can no longer chew or swallow on my own or with someone helping me.

PLACE YOUR INITIALS BY EITHER "YES" OR "NO":

I want to have food and water provided through a tube or an IV if I am permanently unconscious. ____ Yes ____ No

OTHER DIRECTIONS:

Please list any other things you want done or not done.

In addition to the directions I have listed on this form, I also want the following: [specify additional directions]; OR

I do not have any other direction (place your initials here): ____.

SECTION 2. DURABLE POWER OF ATTORNEY FOR HEALTH CARE

APPOINTMENT OF HEALTH CARE AGENT

PLACE YOUR INITIALS BY ONLY ONE OF THE FOLLOWING:

_____ I do not want to name a health care agent (If you initial this answer, go to Section 3).

_____ I do want the person listed below to be my health care agent.

I have talked with this person about my wishes.

First choice for health care agent: [insert name/address/telephone number].

Relationship to me: [specify relationship of health care agent].

FIRST ALTERNATE AGENT

If my first choice for health care agent named above is not able, not willing, or not available to be my health care agent, this is my next choice:

First alternate health care agent: [insert name/address/telephone number].

Relationship to me: [specify relationship of health care agent].

SECOND ALTERNATE AGENT

If neither my first choice for health care agent or my first alternate agent named above are not able, not willing, or not available to be my health care agent, this is my next choice:

Second alternate health care agent: [insert name/address/telephone number].

Relationship to me: [specify relationship of health care agent].

INSTRUCTIONS FOR HEALTH CARE AGENT

PLACE YOUR INITIALS BY EITHER "YES" OR "NO":

I want my health care agent to make decisions about whether to give me food and water through a tube or an IV. _____ Yes _____ No

PLACE YOUR INITIALS BY ONLY ONE OF THE FOLLOWING:

_____ I want my health care agent to follow only the directions as listed on this form.

_____ I want my health care agent to follow my directions as listed on this form and to make any decisions about things I have not covered in the form.

_____ I want my health care agent to make the final decision, even though it could mean doing something different from what I have listed on this form.

SECTION 3. THE THINGS LISTED ON THIS FORM ARE MY DIRECTIONS

I understand the following:

If my doctor or hospital does not want to follow the directions I have listed, they must see that I get to a doctor or hospital who will follow my directions.

If I am pregnant, or if I become pregnant, the choices I have made on this form will not be followed until after the birth of the baby.

If the time comes for me to stop receiving life sustaining treatment or food and water through a tube or an IV, I direct that my doctor talk about the good and bad points of doing this, along with my wishes, with my health care agent, if I have one, and with the following people: [insert names/addresses/telephone numbers].

SECTION 4. SIGNATURE—DECLARANT

Name [insert declarant's name]

Date of Birth [insert month/day/year of birth]

Signed in the presence of the witnesses who have signed below this _____ day of _____, 20__.

SIGNATURE LINE – DECLARANT

SECTION 5. SIGNATURE—WITNESSES

STATEMENT OF WITNESSES

I state this [enter date], under penalty of perjury, that the Declarant has identified (himself/herself) to me and that the Declarant signed or acknowledged this Durable Power of Attorney and Appointment of Health Care Agent in my presence.

I believe the Declarant to be of sound mind, and the Declarant has affirmed (his/her) awareness of the nature of this document and is signing it voluntarily and free from duress. The Declarant requested that I serve as a witness to (his/her) execution of this document.

I declare that I am not related to the Declarant by blood, marriage, or adoption and that to the best of my knowledge I am not entitled to any part of the estate of the Declarant on the death of the principal under a will or by operation of law.

I am not a provider of health or residential care, an employee of a provider of health or residential care, the operator of a community care facility, or an employee of an operator of a health care facility.

I declare that I have no claim against any portion of the estate of the Declarant upon (his/her) death, nor any personal financial responsibility for the payment of Declarant's medical bills or any other of Declarant's obligations.

SIGNATURE LINE/ADDRESS/DATE – WITNESS #1

SIGNATURE LINE/ADDRESS/DATE – WITNESS #2

SIGNATURE LINE/ADDRESS/DATE – WITNESS #3

SECTION 6. ACCEPTANCE BY HEALTH CARE AGENTS

HEALTH CARE AGENT (First Choice)

I, [insert name of health care agent], am willing to serve and accept the appointment as the health care agent for [insert name of declarant] as described in this document.

SIGNATURE LINE/ADDRESS/DATE – HEALTH CARE AGENT

HEALTH CARE AGENT (First Alternate)

I, [insert name of first alternate health care agent], am willing to serve and accept the appointment as the health care agent for [insert name of declarant] as described in this document, if the declarant's first choice cannot serve as health care agent.

SIGNATURE LINE/ADDRESS/DATE – HEALTH CARE AGENT

HEALTH CARE AGENT (Second Alternate)

I, [insert name of second alternate health care agent], am willing to serve and accept the appointment as the health care agent for [insert name of declarant] as described in this document, if neither the declarant's first choice nor first alternate can serve as health care agent.

SIGNATURE LINE/ADDRESS/DATE – HEALTH CARE AGENT (Second Alternate)

NOTARIAL ACKNOWLEDGMENT

BEFORE ME, the undersigned authority, on this day personally appeared [insert name of declarant], and [names of three witnesses], and [names of three health care agents] known to me to be the declarant, witnesses, and health care agents whose names are subscribed to the foregoing instrument in their respective capacities, and, all of said persons being by me duly sworn, [name of declarant] declared to me and to the said witnesses in my presence that said instrument is (his/her) Living Will and Durable Power of Attorney for Health Care, and that (he/she) had willingly and voluntarily made and executed it as (his/her) free act and deed for the purposes therein expressed.

SUBSCRIBED AND SWORN TO BEFORE ME by the declarant, [insert name], by the witnesses [insert names], and by the health care agents [insert names] this _____ day of _____, 20_____.

_____

NOTARY PUBLIC

APPENDIX 9:
THE PATIENT SELF-DETERMINATION ACT OF 1990 [42 U.S.C. 1395 CC (A)]

SUBPART E – MISCELLANEOUS

SEC. 4751. REQUIREMENTS FOR ADVANCED DIRECTIVES UNDER STATE PLANS FOR MEDICAL ASSISTANCE.

(a) IN GENERAL. – Section 1902 (42 U.S.C. 1396a(a)), as amended by sections 4401(a)(2), 4601(d), 4701(a), 4711(a), and 4722 of this title, is amended

(1) in subsection (a)—

(A) by striking "and" at the end of paragraph (55),

(B) by striking the period at the end of paragraph (56) and inserting "; and:, and

(C) by inserting after paragraph (56) the following new paragraphs;

"(57) provide that each hospital, nursing facility, provider of home health care or personal care services, hospice program, or health maintenance organization (as defined in section 1903(m)(1)(A)) receiving funds under the plan shall comply with the requirements of subsection (w);

"(58) provide that the State, acting through a State agency, association, or other private nonprofit entity, develop a written description of the law of State (whether statutory or as recognized by the courts of the State) concerning advance directives that would be distributed by providers or organizations under the requirements of subsection (w)."; and

(2) by adding at the end of the following new subsection:

"(w)(1) For purposes of subsection (a)(57) and sections 1903(m)(1)(A) and 1919(c)(2)(E), the requirements of this sub-section is that a provider or organization (as the case may be) maintained written policies and procedures with respect to all adult individuals receiving medical care by or through the pro-vider or organization—

"(A) to provide written information to each such individual concerning—

"(i) an individual's rights under State law (whether statu-tory or as recognized by the courts of the State) to make decisions concerning such medical care, including the right to accept or refuse medical or surgical treatment and the right to formulate advance directives (as defined in paragraph (3)), and

"(ii) the provider's or organization's written policies re-specting the implementation of such rights;

"(B) to document in the individual's medical record whether or not the individual has executed an advance directive;

"(C) not to condition the provision of care or otherwise discrim-inate against an individual based on whether or not the indi-vidual has executed an advance directive;

"(D) to ensure compliance with requirements of State law (whether statutory or as recognized by the courts of the State) respecting advance directives; and

"(E) to provide (individually or with others) for education for staff and the community on issues concerning advance directives.

Subparagraph (C) shall not be construed as requiring the provision of care which conflicts with an advance directive.

"(2) The written information described in paragraph (1)(A) shall be provided to an adult individual—

"(A) in the case of a hospital, at the time of the individual's ad-mission as an inpatient,

"(B) in the case of a nursing facility, at the time of the individual's admission as a resident,

"(C) in the case of a provider of home health care or personal care services, in advance of the individual coming under the care of the provider,

"(D) in the case of a hospice program, at the time of initial receipt of hospice care by the individual from the program, and

"(E) in the case of a health maintenance organization, at the time of enrollment of the individual with the organization.

"(3) Nothing in this section shall be construed to prohibit the application of a State law which allows for an objection on the basis of conscience for any health care provider or any agent of such provider which as a matter of conscience cannot implement an advance directive."

"(4) In this subsection, the term 'advance directive' means a written instruction, such as a living will or durable power of attorney for health care, recognized under State law (whether statutory or as recognized by the courts of the State) and relating to the provision of such care when the individual is incapacitated.

(a) CONFORMING AMENDMENTS.—

(1) Section 1903(m)(1)(A)(42 U.S.C. 1396b(m)(1)(A)) is amended—

(A) by inserting "meets the requirement of section 1902(w)" after "which" the first place it appears, and

(B) by inserting "meets the requirement of section 1902(a) and" after "which" the second place it appears.

(2) Section 1919(c)(2) of such Act (42 U.S.C. 139r(c)(2)) is amended by adding at the end the following new subparagraph:

"(E) INFORMATION RESPECTING ADVANCE DIRECTIVES.—A nursing facility must comply with the requirements of section 1902(w) (relating to maintaining written policies and procedures respecting advance directives)."

(c) EFFECTIVE DATE.—The amendments made by this section shall apply with respect to services furnished on or after the first day of the first month beginning more than 1 year after the date of the enactment of this Act.

(d) PUBLIC EDUCATION CAMPAIGN.—

(1) IN GENERAL.— The Secretary, no later than 6 months after the date of enactment of this section, shall develop and implement a national campaign to inform the public of the option to execute advance directives and of a patient's right to participate and direct health care decisions.

(2) DEVELOPMENT AND DISTIBUTION OF INFORMATION.— The Secretary shall develop or approve nationwide informational materials that would be distributed by providers under the requirements of this section, to inform the public and the medical and legal profession of each person's right to make decisions concerning medical care, including the right to accept or refuse medical or surgical treatment, and the existence of advance directives.

(3) PROVIDING ASSISTANCE TO STATES.— The Secretary shall assist appropriate State agencies, associations, or other private entities in developing the State-specific documents that would be distributed by providers under the requirements of this section. The Secretary shall further assist appropriate State agencies, associations, or other private entities in ensuring that providers are provided a copy of the documents that are to be distributed under the requirements of the section.

(4) DUTIES OF SECRETARY.— The Secretary shall mail information to Social Security recipients, add a page to the medicare handbook with respect to the provisions of this section.

APPENDIX 10:
THE UNIFORM HEALTH CARE DECISIONS ACT

SECTION 1. DEFINITIONS.

(1) "Advance health-care directive" means an individual instruction or a power of attorney for health care.

(2) "Agent" means an individual designated in a power of attorney for health care to make a health-care decision for the individual granting the power.

(3) "Capacity" means an individual's ability to understand the significant benefits, risks, and alternatives to proposed health care and to make and communicate a health-care decision.

(4) "Guardian" means a judicially appointed guardian or conservator having authority to make a health-care decision for an individual.

(5) "Health care" means any care, treatment, service, or procedure to maintain, diagnose, or otherwise affect an individual's physical or mental condition.

(6) "Health-care decision" means a decision made by an individual or the individual's agent, guardian, or surrogate, regarding the individual's health care, including:

(i) selection and discharge of health-care providers and institutions;

(ii) approval or disapproval of diagnostic tests, surgical procedures, programs of medication, and orders not to resuscitate; and

(iii) directions to provide, withhold, or withdraw artificial nutrition and hydration and all other forms of health care.

(7) "Health-care institution" means an institution, facility, or agency licensed, certified, or otherwise authorized or permitted by law to provide health care in the ordinary course of business.

(8) "Health-care provider" means an individual licensed, certified, or otherwise authorized or permitted by law to provide health care in the ordinary course of business or practice of a profession.

(9) "Individual instruction" means an individual's direction concerning a health-care decision for the individual.

(10) "Person" means an individual, corporation, business trust, estate, trust, partnership, association, joint venture, government, governmental subdivision, agency, or instrumentality, or any other legal or commercial entity.

(11) "Physician" means an individual authorized to practice medicine [or osteopathy] under [appropriate statute].

(12) "Power of attorney for health care" means the designation of an agent to make health-care decisions for the individual granting the power.

(13) "Primary physician" means a physician designated by an individual or the individual's agent, guardian, or surrogate, to have primary responsibility for the individual's health care or, in the absence of a designation or if the designated physician is not reasonably available, a physician who undertakes the responsibility.

(14) "Reasonably available" means readily able to be contacted without undue effort and willing and able to act in a timely manner considering the urgency of the patient's health-care needs.

(15) "State" means a State of the United States, the District of Columbia, the Commonwealth of Puerto Rico, or a territory or insular possession subject to the jurisdiction of the United States.

(16) "Supervising health-care provider" means the primary physician or, if there is no primary physician or the primary physician is not reasonably available, the health-care provider who has undertaken primary responsibility for an individual's health care.

(17) "Surrogate" means an individual, other than a patient's agent or guardian, authorized under this [Act] to make a health-care decision for the patient.

SECTION 2. ADVANCE HEALTH-CARE DIRECTIVES.

(a) An adult or emancipated minor may give an individual instruction. The instruction may be oral or written. The instruction may be limited to take effect only if a specified condition arises.

(b) An adult or emancipated minor may execute a power of attorney for health care, which may authorize the agent to make any health-care decision the principal could have made while having capacity. The power must be in writing and signed by the principal. The power remains in effect notwithstanding the principal's later incapacity and may include individual instructions. Unless related to the principal by blood, marriage, or adoption, an agent may not be an owner, operator, or employee of [a residential long-term health-care institution] at which the principal is receiving care.

(c) Unless otherwise specified in a power of attorney for health care, the authority of an agent becomes effective only upon a determination that the principal lacks capacity, and ceases to be effective upon a determination that the principal has recovered capacity. @PA00N = (d) Unless otherwise specified in a written advance health-care directive, a determination that an individual lacks or has recovered capacity, or that another condition exists that affects an individual instruction or the authority of an agent, must be made by the primary physician.

(e) An agent shall make a health-care decision in accordance with the principal's individual instructions, if any, and other wishes to the extent known to the agent. Otherwise, the agent shall make the decision in accordance with the agent's determination of the principal's best interest. In determining the principal's best interest, the agent shall consider the principal's personal values to the extent known to the agent.

(f) A health-care decision made by an agent for a principal is effective without judicial approval.

(g) A written advance health-care directive may include the individual's nomination of a guardian of the person.

(h) An advance health-care directive is valid for purposes of this [Act] if it complies with this [Act], regardless of when or where executed or communicated.

SECTION 3. REVOCATION OF ADVANCE HEALTH-CARE DIRECTIVE.

(a) An individual may revoke the designation of an agent only by a signed writing or by personally informing the supervising health-care provider.

(b) An individual may revoke all or part of an advance health-care directive, other than the designation of an agent, at any time and in any manner that communicates an intent to revoke.

(c) A health-care provider, agent, guardian, or surrogate who is informed of a revocation shall promptly communicate the fact of the revocation to the supervising health-care provider and to any health-care institution at which the patient is receiving care.

(d) A decree of annulment, divorce, dissolution of marriage, or legal separation revokes a previous designation of a spouse as agent unless otherwise specified in the decree or in a power of attorney for health care.

(e) An advance health-care directive that conflicts with an earlier advance health-care directive revokes the earlier directive to the extent of the conflict.

SECTION 4. OPTIONAL FORM.

The following form may, but need not, be used to create an advance health-care directive. The other sections of this [Act] govern the effect of this or any other writing used to create an advance health-care directive. An individual may complete or modify all or any part of the following form:

ADVANCE HEALTH-CARE DIRECTIVE

Explanation

You have the right to give instructions about your own health care. You also have the right to name someone else to make health-care decisions for you. This form lets you do either or both of these things. It also lets you express your wishes regarding donation of organs and the designation of your primary physician. If you use this form, you may complete or modify all or any part of it. You are free to use a different form.

Part 1 of this form is a power of attorney for health care. Part 1 lets you name another individual as agent to make health-care decisions for you if you become incapable of making your own decisions or if you want someone else to make those decisions for you now even though you are still capable. You may also name an alternate agent to act for you if your first choice is not willing, able, or reasonably available to make decisions for you. Unless related to you, your agent may not be an owner, operator, or employee of [a residential long-term health-care institution] at which you are receiving care.

Unless the form you sign limits the authority of your agent, your agent may make all health-care decisions for you. This form has a place for you to limit the authority of your agent. You need not limit the authority of your agent if you wish to rely on your agent for all health-care decisions that may have to be made. If you choose not to limit the authority of your agent, your agent will have the right to:

(a) consent or refuse consent to any care, treatment, service, or procedure to maintain, diagnose, or otherwise affect a physical or mental condition;

(b) select or discharge health-care providers and institutions;

(c) approve or disapprove diagnostic tests, surgical procedures, programs of medication, and orders not to resuscitate; and

(d) direct the provision, withholding, or withdrawal of artificial nutrition and hydration and all other forms of health care.

Part 2 of this form lets you give specific instructions about any aspect of your health care. Choices are provided for you to express your wishes regarding the provision, withholding, or withdrawal of treatment to keep you alive, including the provision of artificial nutrition and hydration, as well as the provision of pain relief. Space is also provided for you to add to the choices you have made or for you to write out any additional wishes.

Part 3 of this form lets you express an intention to donate your bodily organs and tissues following your death.

Part 4 of this form lets you designate a physician to have primary responsibility for your health care.

After completing this form, sign and date the form at the end. It is recommended but not required that you request two other individuals to sign as witnesses. Give a copy of the signed and completed form to your physician, to any other health-care providers you may have, to any health-care institution at which you are receiving care, and to any health-care agents you have named. You should talk to the person you have named as agent to make sure that he or she understands your wishes and is willing to take the responsibility.

You have the right to revoke this advance health-care directive or replace this form at any time.

PART 1

POWER OF ATTORNEY FOR HEALTH CARE

(1) DESIGNATION OF AGENT: I designate the following individual as my agent to make health-care decisions for me:

_____

(name of individual you choose as agent)

_____

(address) (city) (state) (zip code)

_____

(home phone) (work phone)

OPTIONAL: If I revoke my agent's authority or if my agent is not willing, able, or reasonably available to make a health-care decision for me, I designate as my first alternate agent:

_____

(name of individual you choose as first agent)

_____

(address) (city) (state) (zip code)

_____

(home phone) (work phone)

OPTIONAL: If I revoke the authority of my agent and first alternate agent or if neither is willing, able, or reasonably available to make a health-care decision for me, I designate as my second alternate agent:

_____

(name of individual you choose as second alternate agent)

_____

(address) (city) (state) (zip code)

_____

(home phone) (work phone)

(2) AGENT'S AUTHORITY: My agent is authorized to make all health-care decisions for me, including decisions to provide, withhold, or withdraw artificial nutrition and hydration and all other forms of health care to keep me alive, except as I state here:

_____

_____

_____

(Add additional sheets if needed.)

(3) WHEN AGENT'S AUTHORITY BECOMES EFFECTIVE: My agent's authority becomes effective when my primary physician determines that I am unable to make my own health-care decisions unless I mark the following box.

_____

If I mark this box [ ], my agent's authority to make health-care decisions for me takes effect immediately.

(4) AGENT'S OBLIGATION: My agent shall make health-care decisions for me in accordance with this power of attorney for health care, any instructions I give in Part 2 of this form, and my other wishes to the extent known to my agent. To the extent my wishes are unknown, my agent shall make health-care decisions for me in accordance with what my agent determines to be in my best interest. In determining my best interest, my agent shall consider my personal values to the extent known to my agent.

(5) NOMINATION OF GUARDIAN: If a guardian of my person needs to be appointed for me by a court, I nominate the agent designated in this form. If that agent is not willing, able, or reasonably available to act as guardian, I nominate the alternate agents whom I have named, in the order designated.

PART 2

INSTRUCTIONS FOR HEALTH CARE

If you are satisfied to allow your agent to determine what is best for you in making end-of-life decisions, you need not fill out this part of the form. If you do fill out this part of the form, you may strike any wording you do not want.

(6) END-OF-LIFE DECISIONS: I direct that my health-care providers and others involved in my care provide, withhold, or withdraw treatment in accordance with the choice I have marked below:

[ ] (a) Choice Not To Prolong Life

I do not want my life to be prolonged if

(i) I have an incurable and irreversible condition that will result in my death within a relatively short time,

(ii) I become unconscious and, to a reasonable degree of medical certainty, I will not regain consciousness, or

(iii) the likely risks and burdens of treatment would outweigh the expected benefits, OR

[ ] (b) Choice To Prolong Life

I want my life to be prolonged as long as possible within the limits of generally accepted health-care standards.

(7) ARTIFICIAL NUTRITION AND HYDRATION: Artificial nutrition and hydration must be provided, withheld, or withdrawn in accordance

with the choice I have made in paragraph (6) unless I mark the following box.

If I mark this box [ ], artificial nutrition and hydration must be provided regardless of my condition and regardless of the choice I have made in paragraph (6).

(8) RELIEF FROM PAIN: Except as I state in the following space, I direct that treatment for alleviation of pain or discomfort be provided at all times, even if it hastens my death:

_____

_____

(9) OTHER WISHES: (If you do not agree with any of the optional choices above and wish to write your own, or if you wish to add to the instructions you have given above, you may do so here.) I direct that:

_____

_____

(Add additional sheets if needed.)

PART 3

DONATION OF ORGANS AT DEATH

(OPTIONAL)

(10) Upon my death (mark applicable box)

[ ] (a) I give any needed organs, tissues, or parts, OR

[ ] (b) I give the following organs, tissues, or parts only

_____

(c) My gift is for the following purposes (strike any of the following you do not want)

(i) Transplant

(ii) Therapy

(iii) Research

(iv) Education

PART 4

PRIMARY PHYSICIAN

(OPTIONAL)

(11) I designate the following physician as my primary physician:

_____

(name of physician)

_____

(address) (city) (state) (zip code)

_____

(phone)

OPTIONAL: If the physician I have designated above is not willing, able, or reasonably available to act as my primary physician, I designate the following physician as my primary physician:

_____

(name of physician)

_____

(address) (city) (state) (zip code)

_____

(phone)

(12) EFFECT OF COPY: A copy of this form has the same effect as the original.

(13) SIGNATURES: Sign and date the form here:

_____

(date) (sign your name)

_____

(address) (print your name)

_____

(city) (state)

(Optional) SIGNATURES OF WITNESSES:

First witnessSecond witness

_____

(print name)(print name)

(address)(address)

(city) (state)(city) (state)

(signature of witness)(signature of witness)

(date)(date)

SECTION 5. DECISIONS BY SURROGATE.

(a) A surrogate may make a health-care decision for a patient who is an adult or emancipated minor if the patient has been determined by the primary physician to lack capacity and no agent or guardian has been appointed or the agent or guardian is not reasonably available.

(b) An adult or emancipated minor may designate any individual to act as surrogate by personally informing the supervising health-care provider. In the absence of a designation, or if the designee is not reasonably available, any member of the following classes of the patient's family who is reasonably available, in descending order of priority, may act as surrogate:

(1) the spouse, unless legally separated;

(2) an adult child;

(3) a parent; or

(4) an adult brother or sister.

(c) If none of the individuals eligible to act as surrogate under subsection (b) is reasonably available, an adult who has exhibited special care and concern for the patient, who is familiar with the patient's personal values, and who is reasonably available may act as surrogate.

(d) A surrogate shall communicate his or her assumption of authority as promptly as practicable to the members of the patient's family specified in subsection (b) who can be readily contacted.

(e) If more than one member of a class assumes authority to act as surrogate, and they do not agree on a health-care decision and the supervising health-care provider is so informed, the supervising health-care provider shall comply with the decision of a majority of the members of that class who have communicated their views to the provider. If the class is evenly divided concerning the health-care decision and the supervising health-care provider is so informed, that class and all individuals having lower priority are disqualified from making the decision.

(f) A surrogate shall make a health-care decision in accordance with the patient's individual instructions, if any, and other wishes to the extent known to the surrogate. Otherwise, the surrogate shall make the decision in accordance with the surrogate's determination of the patient's best interest. In determining the patient's best interest, the surrogate shall consider the patient's personal values to the extent known to the surrogate.

(g) A health-care decision made by a surrogate for a patient is effective without judicial approval.

(h) An individual at any time may disqualify another, including a member of the individual's family, from acting as the individual's surrogate by a signed writing or by personally informing the supervising health-care provider of the disqualification.

(i) Unless related to the patient by blood, marriage, or adoption, a surrogate may not be an owner, operator, or employee of [a residential long-term health-care institution] at which the patient is receiving care.

(j) A supervising health-care provider may require an individual claiming the right to act as surrogate for a patient to provide a written declaration under penalty of perjury stating facts and circumstances reasonably sufficient to establish the claimed authority.

SECTION 6. DECISIONS BY GUARDIAN.

(a) A guardian shall comply with the ward's individual instructions and may not revoke the ward's advance health-care directive unless the appointing court expressly so authorizes.

(b) Absent a court order to the contrary, a health-care decision of an agent takes precedence over that of a guardian.

(c) A health-care decision made by a guardian for the ward is effective without judicial approval.

SECTION 7. OBLIGATIONS OF HEALTH-CARE PROVIDER.

(a) Before implementing a health-care decision made for a patient, a supervising health-care provider, if possible, shall promptly communicate to the patient the decision made and the identity of the person making the decision.

(b) A supervising health-care provider who knows of the existence of an advance health-care directive, a revocation of an advance health-care directive, or a designation or disqualification of a surrogate, shall promptly record its existence in the patient's health-care record and, if it is in writing, shall request a copy and if one is furnished shall arrange for its maintenance in the health-care record.

(c) A primary physician who makes or is informed of a determination that a patient lacks or has recovered capacity, or that another condition exists which affects an individual instruction or the authority of an agent, guardian, or surrogate, shall promptly record the determination in the patient's health-care record and communicate the determination to the patient, if possible, and to any person then authorized to make health-care decisions for the patient.

(d) Except as provided in subsections (e) and (f), a health-care provider or institution providing care to a patient shall:

(1) comply with an individual instruction of the patient and with a reasonable interpretation of that instruction made by a person then authorized to make health-care decisions for the patient; and

(2) comply with a health-care decision for the patient made by a person then authorized to make health-care decisions for the patient to the same extent as if the decision had been made by the patient while having capacity.

(e) A health-care provider may decline to comply with an individual instruction or health-care decision for reasons of conscience. A health-care institution may decline to comply with an individual instruction or health-care decision if the instruction or decision is contrary to a policy of the institution which is expressly based on reasons of conscience and if the policy was timely communicated to the patient or to a person then authorized to make health-care decisions for the patient.

(f) A health-care provider or institution may decline to comply with an individual instruction or health-care decision that requires medically ineffective health care or health care contrary to generally accepted health-care standards applicable to the health-care provider or institution.

(g) A health-care provider or institution that declines to comply with an individual instruction or health-care decision shall:

(1) promptly so inform the patient, if possible, and any person then authorized to make health-care decisions for the patient;

(2) provide continuing care to the patient until a transfer can be effected; and

(3) unless the patient or person then authorized to make health-care decisions for the patient refuses assistance, immediately make all reasonable efforts to assist in the transfer of the patient to another health-care provider or institution that is willing to comply with the instruction or decision.

(h) A health-care provider or institution may not require or prohibit the execution or revocation of an advance health-care directive as a condition for providing health care.

SECTION 8. HEALTH-CARE INFORMATION.

Unless otherwise specified in an advance health-care directive, a person then authorized to make health-care decisions for a patient has the same rights as the patient to request, receive, examine, copy, and consent to the disclosure of medical or any other health-care information.

SECTION 9. IMMUNITIES.

(a) A health-care provider or institution acting in good faith and in accordance with generally accepted health-care standards applicable to the health-care provider or institution is not subject to civil or criminal liability or to discipline for unprofessional conduct for:

(1) complying with a health-care decision of a person apparently having authority to make a health-care decision for a patient, including a decision to withhold or withdraw health care;

(2) declining to comply with a health-care decision of a person based on a belief that the person then lacked authority; or

(3) complying with an advance health-care directive and assuming that the directive was valid when made and has not been revoked or terminated.

(b) An individual acting as agent or surrogate under this [Act] is not subject to civil or criminal liability or to discipline for unprofessional conduct for health-care decisions made in good faith.

SECTION 10. STATUTORY DAMAGES.

(a) A health-care provider or institution that intentionally violates this [Act] is subject to liability to the aggrieved individual for damages of $[500] or actual damages resulting from the violation, whichever is greater, plus reasonable attorney's fees.

(b) A person who intentionally falsifies, forges, conceals, defaces, or obliterates an individual's advance health-care directive or a revocation of an advance health-care directive without the individual's consent, or who coerces or fraudulently induces an individual to give, revoke, or not to give an advance health-care directive, is subject to liability to that individual for damages of $[2,500] or actual damages resulting from the action, whichever is greater, plus reasonable attorney's fees.

SECTION 11. CAPACITY.

(a) This [Act] does not affect the right of an individual to make health-care decisions while having capacity to do so.

(b) An individual is presumed to have capacity to make a health-care decision, to give or revoke an advance health-care directive, and to designate or disqualify a surrogate.

SECTION 12. EFFECT OF COPY.

A copy of a written advance health-care directive, revocation of an advance health-care directive, or designation or disqualification of a surrogate has the same effect as the original.

SECTION 13. EFFECT OF [ACT].

(a) This [Act] does not create a presumption concerning the intention of an individual who has not made or who has revoked an advance health-care directive.

(b) Death resulting from the withholding or withdrawal of health care in accordance with this [Act] does not for any purpose constitute a suicide or homicide or legally impair or invalidate a policy of insurance or an annuity providing a death benefit, notwithstanding any term of the policy or annuity to the contrary.

(c) This [Act] does not authorize mercy killing, assisted suicide, euthanasia, or the provision, withholding, or withdrawal of health care, to the extent prohibited by other statutes of this State.

(d) This [Act] does not authorize or require a health-care provider or institution to provide health care contrary to generally accepted health-care standards applicable to the health-care provider or institution.

[(e) This [Act] does not authorize an agent or surrogate to consent to the admission of an individual to a mental health-care institution unless the individual's written advance health-care directive expressly so provides.]

[(f) This [Act] does not affect other statutes of this State governing treatment for mental illness of an individual involuntarily committed to a [mental health-care institution under appropriate statute].]

SECTION 14. JUDICIAL RELIEF.

On petition of a patient, the patient's agent, guardian, or surrogate, a health-care provider or institution involved with the patient's care, or an individual described in Section 5(b) or (c), the [appropriate] court may enjoin or direct a health-care decision or order other equitable relief. A proceeding under this section is governed by [here insert appropriate reference to the rules of procedure or statutory provisions governing expedited proceedings and proceedings affecting incapacitated persons].

SECTION 15. UNIFORMITY OF APPLICATION AND CONSTRUCTION.

This [Act] shall be applied and construed to effectuate its general purpose to make uniform the law with respect to the subject matter of this [Act] among States enacting it.

SECTION 16. SHORT TITLE.

This [Act] may be cited as the Uniform Health-Care Decisions Act.

SECTION 17. SEVERABILITY CLAUSE.

If any provision of this [Act] or its application to any person or circumstance is held invalid, the invalidity does not affect other provisions or applications of this [Act] which can be given effect without the invalid provision or application, and to this end the provisions of this [Act] are severable.

SECTION 18. EFFECTIVE DATE.

SECTION 19. REPEAL.

SOURCE: The National Conference of Commissioners on Uniform State Laws (NCCUSL)

APPENDIX 11:
THE OREGON DEATH WITH DIGNITY ACT

OREGON REVISED STATUTES

(General Provisions)

(Section 1)

Note: The division headings, subdivision headings and leadlines for 127.800 to 127.890, 127.895 and 127.897 were enacted as part of Ballot Measure 16 (1994) and were not provided by Legislative Counsel.

127.800 §1.01. Definitions. The following words and phrases, whenever used in ORS 127.800 to 127.897, have the following meanings:

(1) "Adult" means an individual who is 18 years of age or older.

(2) "Attending physician" means the physician who has primary responsibility for the care of the patient and treatment of the patient's terminal disease.

(3) "Capable" means that in the opinion of a court or in the opinion of the patient's attending physician or consulting physician, psychiatrist or psychologist, a patient has the ability to make and communicate health care decisions to health care providers, including communication through persons familiar with the patient's manner of communicating if those persons are available.

(4) "Consulting physician" means a physician who is qualified by specialty or experience to make a professional diagnosis and prognosis regarding the patient's disease.

(5) "Counseling" means one or more consultations as necessary between a state licensed psychiatrist or psychologist and a patient for the purpose of determining that the patient is capable and not suffering from a psychiatric or psychological disorder or depression causing impaired judgment.

(6) "Health care provider" means a person licensed, certified or otherwise authorized or permitted by the law of this state to administer health care or dispense medication in the ordinary course of business or practice of a profession, and includes a health care facility.

(7) "Informed decision" means a decision by a qualified patient, to request and obtain a prescription to end his or her life in a humane and dignified manner, that is based on an appreciation of the relevant facts and after being fully informed by the attending physician of:

(a) His or her medical diagnosis;

(b) His or her prognosis;

(c) The potential risks associated with taking the medication to be prescribed;

(d) The probable result of taking the medication to be prescribed; and

(e) The feasible alternatives, including, but not limited to, comfort care, hospice care and pain control.

(8) "Medically confirmed" means the medical opinion of the attending physician has been confirmed by a consulting physician who has examined the patient and the patient's relevant medical records.

(9) "Patient" means a person who is under the care of a physician.

(10) "Physician" means a doctor of medicine or osteopathy licensed to practice medicine by the Board of Medical Examiners for the State of Oregon.

(11) "Qualified patient" means a capable adult who is a resident of Oregon and has satisfied the requirements of ORS 127.800 to 127.897 in order to obtain a prescription for medication to end his or her life in a humane and dignified manner.

(12) "Terminal disease" means an incurable and irreversible disease that has been medically confirmed and will, within reasonable medical judgment, produce death within six months. [1995 c.3 §1.01; 1999 c.423 §1]

(Written Request for Medication to End One's Life in a Humane and Dignified Manner)

(Section 2)

127.805 §2.01. Who may initiate a written request for medication.

(1) An adult who is capable, is a resident of Oregon, and has been determined by the attending physician and consulting physician to be suffering from a terminal disease, and who has voluntarily expressed

his or her wish to die, may make a written request for medication for the purpose of ending his or her life in a humane and dignified manner in accordance with ORS 127.800 to 127.897.

(2) No person shall qualify under the provisions of ORS 127.800 to 127.897 solely because of age or disability. [1995 c.3 §2.01; 1999 c.423 §2]

127.810 §2.02. Form of the written request.

(1) A valid request for medication under ORS 127.800 to 127.897 shall be in substantially the form described in ORS 127.897, signed and dated by the patient and witnessed by at least two individuals who, in the presence of the patient, attest that to the best of their knowledge and belief the patient is capable, acting voluntarily, and is not being coerced to sign the request.

(2) One of the witnesses shall be a person who is not:

(a) A relative of the patient by blood, marriage or adoption;

(b) A person who at the time the request is signed would be entitled to any portion of the estate of the qualified patient upon death under any will or by operation of law; or

(c) An owner, operator or employee of a health care facility where the qualified patient is receiving medical treatment or is a resident.

(3) The patient's attending physician at the time the request is signed shall not be a witness.

(4) If the patient is a patient in a long term care facility at the time the written request is made, one of the witnesses shall be an individual designated by the facility and having the qualifications specified by the Department of Human Services by rule. [1995 c.3 §2.02]

(Safeguards)

(Section 3)

127.815 §3.01. Attending physician responsibilities.

(1) The attending physician shall:

(a) Make the initial determination of whether a patient has a terminal disease, is capable, and has made the request voluntarily;

(b) Request that the patient demonstrate Oregon residency pursuant to ORS 127.860;

(c) To ensure that the patient is making an informed decision, inform the patient of:

(A) His or her medical diagnosis;

(B) His or her prognosis;

(C) The potential risks associated with taking the medication to be prescribed;

(D) The probable result of taking the medication to be prescribed; and

(E) The feasible alternatives, including, but not limited to, comfort care, hospice care and pain control;

(d) Refer the patient to a consulting physician for medical confirmation of the diagnosis, and for a determination that the patient is capable and acting voluntarily;

(e) Refer the patient for counseling if appropriate pursuant to ORS 127.825;

(f) Recommend that the patient notify next of kin;

(g) Counsel the patient about the importance of having another person present when the patient takes the medication prescribed pursuant to ORS 127.800 to 127.897 and of not taking the medication in a public place;

(h) Inform the patient that he or she has an opportunity to rescind the request at any time and in any manner, and offer the patient an opportunity to rescind at the end of the 15 day waiting period pursuant to ORS 127.840;

(i) Verify, immediately prior to writing the prescription for medication under ORS 127.800 to 127.897, that the patient is making an informed decision;

(j) Fulfill the medical record documentation requirements of ORS 127.855;

(k) Ensure that all appropriate steps are carried out in accordance with ORS 127.800 to 127.897 prior to writing a prescription for medication to enable a qualified patient to end his or her life in a humane and dignified manner; and

(l)(A) Dispense medications directly, including ancillary medications intended to facilitate the desired effect to minimize the patient's discomfort, provided the attending physician is registered as a dispensing physician with the Board of Medical Examiners, has a current Drug Enforcement Administration certificate and complies with any applicable administrative rule; or

(B) With the patient's written consent:

(i) Contact a pharmacist and inform the pharmacist of the prescription; and

(ii) Deliver the written prescription personally or by mail to the pharmacist, who will dispense the medications to either the patient, the attending physician or an expressly identified agent of the patient.

(2) Notwithstanding any other provision of law, the attending physician may sign the patient's death certificate. [1995 c.3 §3.01; 1999 c.423 §3]

127.820 §3.02. Consulting physician confirmation.

Before a patient is qualified under ORS 127.800 to 127.897, a consulting physician shall examine the patient and his or her relevant medical records and confirm, in writing, the attending physician's diagnosis that the patient is suffering from a terminal disease, and verify that the patient is capable, is acting voluntarily and has made an informed decision. [1995 c.3 §3.02]

127.825 §3.03. Counseling referral.

If in the opinion of the attending physician or the consulting physician a patient may be suffering from a psychiatric or psychological disorder or depression causing impaired judgment, either physician shall refer the patient for counseling. No medication to end a patient's life in a humane and dignified manner shall be prescribed until the person performing the counseling determines that the patient is not suffering from a psychiatric or psychological disorder or depression causing impaired judgment. [1995 c.3 §3.03; 1999 c.423 §4]

127.830 §3.04. Informed decision.

No person shall receive a prescription for medication to end his or her life in a humane and dignified manner unless he or she has made an informed decision as defined in ORS 127.800 (7). Immediately prior to writing a prescription for medication under ORS 127.800 to 127.897, the attending physician shall verify that the patient is making an informed decision. [1995 c.3 §3.04]

127.835 §3.05. Family notification.

The attending physician shall recommend that the patient notify the next of kin of his or her request for medication pursuant to ORS 127.800 to 127.897. A patient who declines or is unable to notify next of kin shall not have his or her request denied for that reason. [1995 c.3 §3.05; 1999 c.423 §6]

127.840 §3.06. Written and oral requests.

In order to receive a prescription for medication to end his or her life in a humane and dignified manner, a qualified patient shall have made an oral request and a written request, and reiterate the oral request to his or her attending physician no less than fifteen (15) days after making the initial oral request. At the time the qualified patient makes his or her second oral request, the attending physician shall offer the patient an opportunity to rescind the request. [1995 c.3 §3.06]

127.845 §3.07. Right to rescind request.

A patient may rescind his or her request at any time and in any manner without regard to his or her mental state. No prescription for medication under ORS 127.800 to 127.897 may be written without the attending physician offering the qualified patient an opportunity to rescind the request. [1995 c.3 §3.07]

127.850 §3.08. Waiting periods.

No less than fifteen (15) days shall elapse between the patient's initial oral request and the writing of a prescription under ORS 127.800 to 127.897. No less than 48 hours shall elapse between the patient's written request and the writing of a prescription under ORS 127.800 to 127.897. [1995 c.3 §3.08]

127.855 §3.09. Medical record documentation requirements.

The following shall be documented or filed in the patient's medical record:

(1) All oral requests by a patient for medication to end his or her life in a humane and dignified manner;

(2) All written requests by a patient for medication to end his or her life in a humane and dignified manner;

(3) The attending physician's diagnosis and prognosis, determination that the patient is capable, acting voluntarily and has made an informed decision;

(4) The consulting physician's diagnosis and prognosis, and verification that the patient is capable, acting voluntarily and has made an informed decision;

(5) A report of the outcome and determinations made during counseling, if performed;

(6) The attending physician's offer to the patient to rescind his or her request at the time of the patient's second oral request pursuant to ORS 127.840; and

(7) A note by the attending physician indicating that all requirements under ORS 127.800 to 127.897 have been met and indicating the steps taken to carry out the request, including a notation of the medication prescribed. [1995 c.3 §3.09]

127.860 §3.10. Residency requirement.

Only requests made by Oregon residents under ORS 127.800 to 127.897 shall be granted. Factors demonstrating Oregon residency include but are not limited to:

(1) Possession of an Oregon driver license;

(2) Registration to vote in Oregon;

(3) Evidence that the person owns or leases property in Oregon; or

(4) Filing of an Oregon tax return for the most recent tax year. [1995 c.3 §3.10; 1999 c.423 §8]

127.865 §3.11. Reporting requirements.

(1)(a) The Department of Human Services shall annually review a sample of records maintained pursuant to ORS 127.800 to 127.897.

(b) The department shall require any health care provider upon dispensing medication pursuant to ORS 127.800 to 127.897 to file a copy of the dispensing record with the department.

(2) The department shall make rules to facilitate the collection of information regarding compliance with ORS 127.800 to 127.897. Except as otherwise required by law, the information collected shall not be a public record and may not be made available for inspection by the public.

(3) The department shall generate and make available to the public an annual statistical report of information collected under subsection (2) of this section. [1995 c.3 §3.11; 1999 c.423 §9; 2001 c.104 §40]

127.870 §3.12. Effect on construction of wills, contracts and statutes.

(1) No provision in a contract, will or other agreement, whether written or oral, to the extent the provision would affect whether a person may make or rescind a request for medication to end his or her life in a humane and dignified manner, shall be valid.

(2) No obligation owing under any currently existing contract shall be conditioned or affected by the making or rescinding of a request, by a person, for medication to end his or her life in a humane and dignified manner. [1995 c.3 §3.12]

127.875 §3.13. Insurance or annuity policies.

The sale, procurement, or issuance of any life, health, or accident insurance or annuity policy or the rate charged for any policy shall not be conditioned upon or affected by the making or rescinding of a request, by a person, for medication to end his or her life in a humane and dignified manner. Neither shall a qualified patient's act of ingesting medication to end his or her life in a humane and dignified manner have an effect upon a life, health, or accident insurance or annuity policy. [1995 c.3 §3.13]

127.880 §3.14. Construction of Act.

Nothing in ORS 127.800 to 127.897 shall be construed to authorize a physician or any other person to end a patient's life by lethal injection, mercy killing or active euthanasia. Actions taken in accordance with ORS 127.800 to 127.897 shall not, for any purpose, constitute suicide, assisted suicide, mercy killing or homicide, under the law. [1995 c.3 §3.14]

(Immunities and Liabilities)

(Section 4)

127.885 §4.01. Immunities; basis for prohibiting health care provider from participation; notification; permissible sanctions. Except as provided in ORS 127.890:

(1) No person shall be subject to civil or criminal liability or professional disciplinary action for participating in good faith compliance with ORS 127.800 to 127.897. This includes being present when a qualified patient takes the prescribed medication to end his or her life in a humane and dignified manner.

(2) No professional organization or association, or health care provider, may subject a person to censure, discipline, suspension, loss of license, loss of privileges, loss of membership or other penalty for participating or refusing to participate in good faith compliance with ORS 127.800 to 127.897.

(3) No request by a patient for or provision by an attending physician of medication in good faith compliance with the provisions of ORS 127.800 to 127.897 shall constitute neglect for any purpose of law or provide the sole basis for the appointment of a guardian or conservator.

(4) No health care provider shall be under any duty, whether by contract, by statute or by any other legal requirement to participate in the provision to a qualified patient of medication to end his or her life in a humane and dignified manner. If a health care provider is unable or unwilling to carry out a patient's request under ORS 127.800 to 127.897, and the patient transfers his or her care to a new health care

provider, the prior health care provider shall transfer, upon request, a copy of the patient's relevant medical records to the new health care provider.

(5)(a) Notwithstanding any other provision of law, a health care provider may prohibit another health care provider from participating in ORS 127.800 to 127.897 on the premises of the prohibiting provider if the prohibiting provider has notified the health care provider of the prohibiting provider's policy regarding participating in ORS 127.800 to 127.897. Nothing in this paragraph prevents a health care provider from providing health care services to a patient that do not constitute participation in ORS 127.800 to 127.897.

(b) Notwithstanding the provisions of subsections (1) to (4) of this section, a health care provider may subject another health care provider to the sanctions stated in this paragraph if the sanctioning health care provider has notified the sanctioned provider prior to participation in ORS 127.800 to 127.897 that it prohibits participation in ORS 127.800 to 127.897:

(A) Loss of privileges, loss of membership or other sanction provided pursuant to the medical staff bylaws, policies and procedures of the sanctioning health care provider if the sanctioned provider is a member of the sanctioning provider's medical staff and participates in ORS 127.800 to 127.897 while on the health care facility premises, as defined in ORS 442.015, of the sanctioning health care provider, but not including the private medical office of a physician or other provider;

(B) Termination of lease or other property contract or other nonmonetary remedies provided by lease contract, not including loss or restriction of medical staff privileges or exclusion from a provider panel, if the sanctioned provider participates in ORS 127.800 to 127.897 while on the premises of the sanctioning health care provider or on property that is owned by or under the direct control of the sanctioning health care provider; or

(C) Termination of contract or other nonmonetary remedies provided by contract if the sanctioned provider participates in ORS 127.800 to 127.897 while acting in the course and scope of the sanctioned provider's capacity as an employee or independent contractor of the sanctioning health care provider. Nothing in this subparagraph shall be construed to prevent:

(i) A health care provider from participating in ORS 127.800 to 127.897 while acting outside the course and scope of the provider's capacity as an employee or independent contractor; or

(ii) A patient from contracting with his or her attending physician and consulting physician to act outside the course and scope of the provider's capacity as an employee or independent contractor of the sanctioning health care provider.

(c) A health care provider that imposes sanctions pursuant to paragraph (b) of this subsection must follow all due process and other procedures the sanctioning health care provider may have that are related to the imposition of sanctions on another health care provider.

(d) For purposes of this subsection:

(A) "Notify" means a separate statement in writing to the health care provider specifically informing the health care provider prior to the provider's participation in ORS 127.800 to 127.897 of the sanctioning health care provider's policy about participation in activities covered by ORS 127.800 to 127.897.

(B) "Participate in ORS 127.800 to 127.897" means to perform the duties of an attending physician pursuant to ORS 127.815, the consulting physician function pursuant to ORS 127.820 or the counseling function pursuant to ORS 127.825. "Participate in ORS 127.800 to 127.897" does not include:

(i) Making an initial determination that a patient has a terminal disease and informing the patient of the medical prognosis;

(ii) Providing information about the Oregon Death with Dignity Act to a patient upon the request of the patient;

(iii) Providing a patient, upon the request of the patient, with a referral to another physician; or

(iv) A patient contracting with his or her attending physician and consulting physician to act outside of the course and scope of the provider's capacity as an employee or independent contractor of the sanctioning health care provider.

(6) Suspension or termination of staff membership or privileges under subsection (5) of this section is not reportable under ORS 441.820. Action taken pursuant to ORS 127.810, 127.815, 127.820 or 127.825 shall not be the sole basis for a report of unprofessional or dishonorable conduct under ORS 677.415 (2) or (3).

(7) No provision of ORS 127.800 to 127.897 shall be construed to allow a lower standard of care for patients in the community where the patient is treated or a similar community. [1995 c.3 §4.01; 1999 c.423 §10]

Note: As originally enacted by the people, the leadline to section 4.01 read "Immunities." The remainder of the leadline was added by editorial action.

127.890 §4.02. Liabilities.

(1) A person who without authorization of the patient willfully alters or forges a request for medication or conceals or destroys a rescission of that request with the intent or effect of causing the patient's death shall be guilty of a Class A felony.

(2) A person who coerces or exerts undue influence on a patient to request medication for the purpose of ending the patient's life, or to destroy a rescission of such a request, shall be guilty of a Class A felony.

(3) Nothing in ORS 127.800 to 127.897 limits further liability for civil damages resulting from other negligent conduct or intentional misconduct by any person.

(4) The penalties in ORS 127.800 to 127.897 do not preclude criminal penalties applicable under other law for conduct which is inconsistent with the provisions of ORS 127.800 to 127.897. [1995 c.3 §4.02]

127.892 Claims by governmental entity for costs incurred.

Any governmental entity that incurs costs resulting from a person terminating his or her life pursuant to the provisions of ORS 127.800 to 127.897 in a public place shall have a claim against the estate of the person to recover such costs and reasonable attorney fees related to enforcing the claim. [1999 c.423 §5a]

(Severability)

(Section 5)

127.895 §5.01. Severability.

Any section of ORS 127.800 to 127.897 being held invalid as to any person or circumstance shall not affect the application of any other section of ORS 127.800 to 127.897 which can be given full effect without the invalid section or application. [1995 c.3 §5.01]

(Form of the Request)

(Section 6)

127.897 §6.01. Form of the request.

A request for a medication as authorized by ORS 127.800 to 127.897 shall be in substantially the following form:

REQUEST FOR MEDICATION TO END MY LIFE IN A HUMANE AND DIGNIFIED MANNER

I, _____, am an adult of sound mind. I am suffering from _____, which my attending physician has determined is a terminal disease and which has been medically confirmed by a consulting physician. I have been fully informed of my diagnosis, prognosis, the nature of medication to be prescribed and potential associated risks, the expected result, and the feasible alternatives, including comfort care, hospice care and pain control. I request that my attending physician prescribe medication that will end my life in a humane and dignified manner.

INITIAL ONE:

_____ I have informed my family of my decision and taken their opinions into consideration.

_____ I have decided not to inform my family of my decision.

_____ I have no family to inform of my decision.

I understand that I have the right to rescind this request at any time. I understand the full import of this request and I expect to die when I take the medication to be prescribed. I further understand that although most deaths occur within three hours, my death may take longer and my physician has counseled me about this possibility. I make this request voluntarily and without reservation, and I accept full moral responsibility for my actions.

Signed: _____ Dated: _____

DECLARATION OF WITNESSES

We declare that the person signing this request:

(a) Is personally known to us or has provided proof of identity;

(b) Signed this request in our presence;

(c) Appears to be of sound mind and not under duress, fraud or undue influence;

(d) Is not a patient for whom either of us is attending physician.

_____Witness 1/Date

_____Witness 2/Date

NOTE: One witness shall not be a relative (by blood, marriage or adoption) of the person signing this request, shall not be entitled to any portion of the person's estate upon death and shall not own, operate or be employed at a health care facility where the person is a patient or resident. If the patient is an inpatient at a health care facility, one of the witnesses shall be an individual designated by the facility.

––––––––––––––––––––

[1995 c.3 §6.01; 1999 c.423 §11]

PENALTIES

127.990: [Formerly part of 97.990; repealed by 1993 c.767 §29]

127.995 Penalties.

(1) It shall be a Class A felony for a person without authorization of the principal to willfully alter, forge, conceal or destroy an instrument, the reinstatement or revocation of an instrument or any other evidence or document reflecting the principal's desires and interests, with the intent and effect of causing a withholding or withdrawal of life-sustaining procedures or of artificially administered nutrition and hydration which hastens the death of the principal.

(2) Except as provided in subsection (1) of this section, it shall be a Class A misdemeanor for a person without authorization of the principal to willfully alter, forge, conceal or destroy an instrument, the reinstatement or revocation of an instrument, or any other evidence or document reflecting the principal's desires and interests with the intent or effect of affecting a health care decision. [Formerly 127.585]

APPENDIX 12:
PATIENT REQUEST FOR MEDICATION UNDER *THE OREGON DEATH WITH DIGNITY ACT*

REQUEST FOR MEDICATION
TO END MY LIFE IN A HUMANE AND DIGNIFIED MANNER

I, _____, am an adult of sound mind.
     First   Middle   Last

I am suffering from _____, which my attending/prescribing physician has determined is a terminal disease and which has been medically confirmed by a consulting physician.

I have been fully informed of: my diagnosis; prognosis; the nature of medication to be prescribed and potential associated risks; the expected result; and feasible alternatives, including comfort care, hospice care and pain control.

I request that my attending/prescribing physician prescribe medication that will end my life in a humane and dignified manner and also contact any pharmacist to fill the prescription.

Initial One

[   ] I have informed my family of my decision and taken their opinions into consideration.

[   ] I have decided not to inform my family of my decision.

[   ] I have no family to inform of my decision.

I understand that I have the right to rescind this request at any time.

I understand the full import of this request and I expect to die when I take the medication to be prescribed.

I make this request voluntarily and without reservation, and I accept full moral responsibility for my actions.

I further understand that although most deaths occur within three hours, my death may take longer and my physician has counseled me about this possibility.

Signature:	County of Residence:	Date:

DECLARATION OF WITNESSES

By *initialing* and *signing* below, we declare that the person making and signing the above request:

Witness 1   Witness 2

[ ] [ ] 1. Is personally known to us or has provided proof of identity;

[ ] [ ] 2. **Signed this request <u>in our presence</u> on the date following the person's signature;**

[ ] [ ] 3. Appears to be of sound mind and not under duress, fraud or undue influence;

[ ] [ ] 4. Is not a patient for whom either of us is the attending physician.

Printed Name:	Signature:	Date:
Witness 1		
Printed Name:	Signature:	Date:
Witness 2		

NOTE: One witness shall not be a relative (by blood, marriage or adoption) of the person signing this request, shall not be entitled to any portion of the person's estate upon death and shall not own, operate or be employed at a health care facility where the person is a patient or resident. If the patient is an inpatient at a long-term health care facility, one of the witnesses shall be an individual designated by the facility.

Copies of this form are available at http://egov.oregon.gov/DHS/ph/pas/index.shtml.   Rev. 04/06

APPENDIX 13:
ATTENDING PHYSICIAN'S COMPLIANCE FORM UNDER *THE OREGON DEATH WITH DIGNITY ACT*

SEND A COPY OF THIS FORM TO OREGON HEALTH SERVICES
ATTENDING PHYSICIAN'S COMPLIANCE FORM
ORS 127.800 - ORS 127.897
MAIL FORM TO: Oregon Health Services, Center for Health Statistics
P.O. Box 14050, Portland, OR 97293-0050

PLEASE PRINT

A	PATIENT INFORMATION	
PATIENT'S NAME (LAST, FIRST, M.I.)		DATE OF BIRTH:
MEDICAL DIAGNOSIS		

B	PHYSICIAN INFORMATION	
NAME (LAST, FIRST, M.I.)		TELEPHONE NUMBER (　　　) 　—
MAILING ADDRESS		
CITY, STATE AND ZIP CODE		

C	ACTION TAKEN TO COMPLY WITH LAW	
1. FIRST ORAL REQUEST		
First oral request for medication to end life.		DATE
Comments:		

Indicate compliance by checking the boxes. (Both the attending and consulting physicians must make these determinations.)

☐ 1. Determination that the patient has a terminal disease.
☐ 2. Determination the patient has six months or less to live.
☐ 3. Determination that patient is capable.**
☐ 4. Determination that patient is an Oregon resident.***
☐ 5. Determination that patient is acting voluntarily.

6. Determination that patient has made his/her decision after being fully informed of:

☐ a) His or her medical diagnosis; and
☐ b) His or her prognosis; and
☐ c) The potential risks associated with taking the medication to be prescribed; and
☐ d) The potential result of taking the medication to be prescribed; and
☐ e) The feasible alternatives, including, but not limited to, comfort care, hospice care and pain control.

Indicate compliance by checking the boxes.　　　　DATE:

☐ 1. Patient informed of his or her right to rescind the request at any time.
☐ 2. Patient recommended to inform next of kin.
☐ 3. Patient counseled about the importance of having another person present when the patient takes the medication(s).
☐ 4. Patient counseled about the importance of not taking the medication in a public place.

2. SECOND ORAL REQUEST (*Must be made **15 days** or more after the first oral request.*)

Indicate compliance by checking the boxes.　　　　DATE:

☐ 1. Second oral request for medication to end life.
☐ 2. Patient informed of the right to rescind the request at any time.

Comments:

Rev. 09/06

Health Care Directives　　　　　　　　　　　　　　　　　　　**119**

SEND A COPY OF THIS FORM TO OREGON HEALTH SERVICES
ATTENDING PHYSICIAN'S COMPLIANCE FORM (continued)

PATIENT INFORMATION	
PATIENT'S NAME (LAST, FIRST, M.I.)	DATE OF BIRTH

C — ACTION TAKEN TO COMPLY WITH THE LAW – continued

3. PATIENT'S WRITTEN REQUEST

☐ Written request for medication to end life received. Please attach request. (*No less than 48 hours shall elapse between the written request and writing the prescription.*)   DATE

Comments:

D — MEDICAL CONSULTATION (Attach consultant's form.)

Medical consultation and second opinion requested from:

MEDICAL CONSULTANT'S NAME	TELEPHONE NUMBER ( ) —	DATE

E — PSYCHIATRIC/PSYCHOLOGICAL EVALUATION

Check one of the following (required):

☐ I have determined that the patient is not suffering from a psychiatric or psychological disorder, or depression, causing impaired judgment, in accordance with ORS 127.825.

☐ I have referred the patient to the provider listed below for evaluation and counseling for a possible psychiatric or psychological disorder, or depression causing impaired judgment, **and attached the consultant's form.**

PSYCHIATRIC CONSULTANT'S NAME	TELEPHONE NUMBER ( ) —	DATE

F — MEDICATION PRESCRIBED AND INFORMATION PROVIDED TO PATIENT

(*To be prescribed no sooner than 48 hours after patient's written request has been signed.*)

Lethal medication prescribed *and dose*	DATE PRESCRIBED

Please check one of the following:

☐ Dispensed medication directly. **Date** ___/___/___

☐ Contacted pharmacist and delivered prescription personally or by mail to the pharmacist.
Pharmacy Name   City   Phone # ( )   -

Immediately prior to writing the prescription, the patient was fully informed of: (*check boxes*)

☐ (a) his or her medical diagnosis;

☐ (b) his or her prognosis;

☐ (c) the potential risks associated with taking the medication to be prescribed;

☐ (d) the probable result of taking the medication to be prescribed;

☐ (e) the feasible alternatives, including, but not limited to, comfort care, hospice care and pain control.

To the best of my knowledge, all of the requirements under the Death with Dignity Act have been met.

✗ PHYSICIAN'S SIGNATURE	DATE

* If comments in any section exceed the space provided, please use an attached page. Supplemental comments should be identified using the appropriate alpha-numeric notation (e.g., C3).

** "Capable" means that in the opinion of a court, or in the opinion of the patient's attending physician or consulting physician, a patient has the ability to make and communicate health care decisions to health care providers, including communication through persons familiar with the patient's manner of communicating, if those persons are available.

*** Factors demonstrating residency include, but are not limited to: 1) Possession of an Oregon driver's license; 2) Registration to vote in Oregon; 3) Evidence that a person leases/owns property in Oregon; or 4) Filing of an Oregon tax return for the most recent tax year. Only the attending physician is required to affirm Oregon residency.

*Note: Besides this form, **it is the attending physician's responsibility** to send the following documents to Health Services: 1) Patient's written request; 2) Consulting physician's report; and 3) Psychiatric evaluation referral report (if performed).*

This form is revised periodically. To assure that you are using the most current version, please refer to:
http://egov.oregon.gov/DHS/ph/pas/index.shtml

Rev. 09/06

APPENDIX 14:
STATEMENT REGARDING ANATOMICAL GIFTS

I, [insert donor's name and address], make the following statement regarding anatomical gifts.

ANATOMICAL GIFT

I give such parts of my body to such individuals, institutions, or physicians, qualified to receive anatomical gifts under [specify applicable section of the Uniform Anatomical Gifts Act or the state law governing anatomical gifts], as may be requested by such individuals, institutions, or physicians. I request that my personal representative or an authorized person make anatomical gifts in a manner consistent with my desires expressed in this statement, and I request that my next of kin respect my wishes.

PRIORITY OF DONATIONS

An anatomical gift that will be used in connection with the treatment of an imminently life threatening disorder shall take precedence over a gift of that part to any other donee. My personal representative or an authorized person shall make final determination of who is to receive any part if a conflict should arise.

ATTENDING PHYSICIAN

If my attending physician accepts an anatomical gift on behalf of a donee, that physician shall not participate in the procedure for removing or transplanting such part.

INSTRUCTIONS

If I have given any written instructions regarding the burial, cremation, or other disposition of my body, I direct that any donee take possession of my body subject to such instructions, if that donee has actual knowledge of such instructions. If there is any conflict between the statements made in this document and such instructions, my wishes regarding anatomical gifts shall take preference over my instructions regarding the disposition of my body.

COUNTERPARTS

I may be signing more than one statement regarding anatomical gifts. I intend that only signed documents be effective and that no effect shall be given to a photocopy or other reproduction of a signed document.

DEFINITIONS

The term "part," "physician," and "attending physician" have the same meaning as is given to these terms in the [specify applicable section of the Uniform Anatomical Gifts Act or the state law governing anatomical gifts]. The term "authorized person" means a person authorized to make donations under [specify applicable section of the Uniform Anatomical Gifts Act or the state law governing anatomical gifts], in the order of priority provided in that statute.

EXPENSES

I make this gift on the condition that the gift be made at no expense to my estate or my family. All expenses or costs associated with the gift shall be borne by the donee or recipient or an individual or entity on the donee's or recipient's behalf.

Signed in the presence of the witnesses who have signed below this _____ day of _____, 20__.

SIGNATURE LINE – DONOR

NOTARIAL ACKNOWLEDGMENT

BEFORE ME, the undersigned authority, on this day personally appeared [insert name of donor], and [names of two witnesses], known to me to be the declarant and witnesses whose names are subscribed to the foregoing instrument in their respective capacities, and, all of said persons being by me duly sworn, [name of donor] declared to me and to the said witnesses in my presence that said instrument is (his/her) Statement Regarding Anatomical Gifts, and that (he/she) had willingly and voluntarily made and executed it as (his/her) free act and deed for the purposes therein expressed.

SUBSCRIBED AND SWORN TO BEFORE ME by the declarant, [insert name] and by the witnesses [insert names] this _____ day of _____, 20_____.

_____

NOTARY PUBLIC

APPENDIX 15:
SAMPLE ORGAN/TISSUE DONOR CARD

Organ/Tissue Donor Card

I wish to donate my organs and tissues. I wish to give:

☐ any needed organs and tissues

☐ only the following organs and tissues:

Donor
Signature _____ Date _____

Witness _____

Witness _____

GLOSSARY

Acknowledgement—A formal declaration of one's signature before a notary public.

Active Euthanasia—The inducement of gentle death solely by means without which life would continue naturally.

Advance directive—A written document that expresses an individual's preferences and instructions regarding health care in the event the individual becomes incompetent or unable to communicate or loses decision-making abilities.

Affidavit—A sworn or affirmed statement made in writing and signed; if sworn, it is notarized.

Agent—An individual designated in a power of attorney for health care to make a health-care decision for the individual granting the power.

Allocation—The system of ensuring that organs and tissues are distributed fairly to patients who are in need.

American Bar Association (ABA)—A national organization of lawyers and law students.

American Civil Liberties Union (ACLU)—A nationwide organization dedicated to the enforcement and preservation of rights and civil liberties guaranteed by the federal and state constitutions.

Anatomical Donation—The act of giving one's organs or tissue to someone else.

Artificial Nutrition and Hydration—Food, water or other fluids that are artificially administered.

Attending Physician—The doctor who is the primary caregiver for a particular patient.

Attestation—The act of witnessing an instrument in writing at the request of the party making the same, and subscribing it as a witness.

Attorney-in-fact—The person named to serve under a durable power of attorney to make medical, financial or personal decisions for someone who is unable to do so.

Beneficiary—A person who is designated to receive property upon the death of another, such as the beneficiary of a life insurance policy, who receives the proceeds upon the death of the insured.

Benefits and Burdens—A commonly used guideline for deciding whether or not to withhold or withdraw medical treatments.

Bequest—Refers to a gift of personal property contained in a will.

Best Interest—In the context of refusal of medical treatment or end-of-life court opinions, a standard for making health care decisions based on what others believe to be "best" for a patient by weighing the benefits and the burdens of continuing, withholding or withdrawing treatment.

Bill of Rights—The first eight amendments to the United States Constitution.

Brain Death—Occurs when a person's brain activity stops permanently after which it is impossible to return to life.

Capacity—In relation to end-of-life decision-making, a patient has medical decision making capacity if he or she has the ability to understand the medical problem and the risks and benefits of the available treatment options.

Cardiopulmonary Resuscitation—Cardiopulmonary resuscitation (CPR) is a group of treatments used when someone's heart and/or breathing stops in an attempt to restart the heart and breathing, including mouth-to-mouth breathing, pressing on the chest to mimic the heart's function and cause blood to circulate, electric shock, and heart-stimulating drugs.

Clear and Convincing Evidence—A high measure or degree of proof that may be required legally to prove a patient's wishes.

Codicil—A document modifying an existing will which, in order to be valid, must be formally drafted and witnessed according to statutory requirements.

Competent Adult—An adult who is alert, capable of understanding a lay description of medical procedures and able to appreciate the consequences of providing, withholding, or withdrawing medical procedures.

Conservator—A conservator is the court-appointed custodian of property belonging to a person determined to be unable to properly manage his or her property.

Constitution—The fundamental principles of law which frame a governmental system.

Constitutional Right—Refers to the individual liberties granted by the constitution of a state or the federal government.

Co-payment—The amount the insured may have to pay each time they receive services under their health plan

Coroner—The public official whose responsibility it is to investigate the circumstances and causes of deaths which occur within his or her jurisdiction.

Decedent—A deceased person.

Decree—A decision or order of the court.

Discharge Plan—A plan which describes the arrangements for any health care services a patient may need after leaving the hospital.

Do-Not-Resuscitate (DNR) Order—A DNR order is a physician's written order instructing health care providers not to attempt cardiopulmonary resuscitation (CPR) in case of cardiac or respiratory arrest.

Due Process Rights—All rights which are of such fundamental importance as to require compliance with due process standards of fairness and justice.

Durable Power of Attorney for Health Care—Also known as a "health care proxy," refers to a document naming a person to make medical decisions in the event that the individual becomes unable to make those decisions himself or herself.

Duress—Refers to the action of one person which compels another to do something he or she would not otherwise do.

Duty—The obligation, to which the law will give recognition and effect, to conform to a particular standard of conduct toward another.

Emergency Medical Services (EMS)—A group of governmental and private agencies that employ paramedics, first responders, and other ambulance crew to provide emergency care to persons outside of health care facilities.

End-Stage Organ Disease—A disease that ultimately leads to functional failure of an organ, e.g., emphysema (lungs), cardiomyopathy (heart), and polycystic kidney disease (kidneys).

End-stage renal disease (ESRD)—A very serious and life-threatening kidney disease which is treated by dialysis and kidney transplantation.

Euthanasia—The act of painlessly assisting in the death of a person suffering from terminal illness or other prolonged suffering. Literally means "good death" in Greek.

Execution—The performance of all acts necessary to render a written instrument complete, such as signing, sealing, acknowledging, and delivering the instrument.

Fraud—A false representation of a matter of fact, whether by words or by conduct, by false or misleading allegations, or by concealment of that which should have been disclosed, which deceives and is intended to deceive another, and thereby causes injury to that person.

Guardian—A judicially appointed guardian or conservator having authority to make a health-care decision for an individual.

Guardian Ad Litem—Person appointed by a court to represent a minor or incompetent for purpose of some litigation.

Health Care—Any care, treatment, service, or procedure to maintain, diagnose, or otherwise affect an individual's physical or mental condition.

Health Care Agent—The person named in an advance directive or as permitted under state law to make health care decisions on behalf of a person who is no longer able to make medical decisions.

Health Care Decision—A decision made by an individual or the individual's agent, guardian, or surrogate, regarding the individual's health care, including: (1) selection and discharge of health-care providers and institutions; (2) approval or disapproval of diagnostic tests, surgical procedures, programs of medication, and orders not to resuscitate; and (3) directions to provide, withhold, or withdraw artificial nutrition and hydration and all other forms of health care.

Health Care Institution—An institution, facility, or agency licensed, certified, or otherwise authorized or permitted by law to provide health care in the ordinary course of business.

Health Care Provider—A person who is licensed, certified, registered, or otherwise authorized by law to administer or provide health care in the ordinary course of business or in the practice of a profession.

Health Care Proxy—Any person lawfully designated to act on behalf of an individual.

Hospice Care—A program model for delivering palliative care to individuals who are in the final stages of terminal illness.

Illegal—Against the law.

Incapacity—Incapacity is a defense to breach of contract which refers to a lack of legal, physical or intellectual power to enter into a contract.

Incompetency—Lack of legal qualification or fitness to discharge a legally required duty or to handle one's own affairs; also refers to matters not admissible in evidence.

Informed Consent—The requirement that a patient be apprised of the nature and risks of a medical procedure before the physician can validly claim exemption from liability for battery, or from responsibility for medical complications.

Intubation—Refers to "endotracheal intubation"—i.e., the insertion of a tube through the mouth or nose into the trachea to create and maintain an open airway to assist breathing.

Legal Aid—A national organization established to provide legal services to those who are unable to afford private representation.

Legal Capacity—Referring to the legal capacity to sue, it is the requirement that a person bringing the lawsuit have a sound mind, be of lawful age, and be under no restraint or legal disability.

Legislation—Laws enacted by state or federal representatives.

Life Expectancy—The period of time which a person is statistically expected to live, based on such factors as their present age and sex.

Life Insurance—A contract between an insured and an insurer whereby the insurer promises to pay a sum of money upon the death of the insured to his or her designated beneficiary, in return for the periodic payment of money, known as a premium.

Life-Sustaining Treatment—Any medical treatment, procedure, or intervention that, in the judgment of the attending physician, when applied to the patient, would serve only to prolong the dying process where the patient has a terminal illness or injury, or would serve only to maintain the patient in a condition of permanent unconsciousness.

Living Will—A declaration that states an individual's wishes concerning the use of extraordinary life support systems.

Long Term Care—The services provided at home or in an institutionalized setting to older persons who require medical or personal care for an extended period of time.

Mechanical ventilation—Mechanical ventilation is used to support or replace the function of the lungs by use of a machine called a ventilator that forces air into the lungs.

Medicaid—A federal program, financed by federal, state and local governments, intended to provide access to health care services for the poor.

Medical Malpractice—The failure of a physician to exercise that degree of skill and learning commonly applied under all the circumstances in the community by the average prudent reputable professional in the same field.

Medicare—The program governed by the Social Security Administration to provide medical and hospital coverage to the aged or disabled.

Minor—A person who has not yet reached the age of legal competence, which is designated as 18 in most states.

Narcotics—Generic term for any drug which dulls the senses or induces sleep and which commonly becomes addictive after prolonged use.

Notice of Petition—Written notice of a petitioner that a hearing will be held in a court to determine the relief requested in an annexed petition.

Oath—A sworn declaration of the truth under penalty of perjury.

Ombudsman—Under certain state laws, an individual licensed to oversee various health care issues.

Out-of-Pocket Maximum—Refers to the maximum amount an insured may have to pay in coinsurance payments for covered services under the plan each year before the plan begins paying the full amount of covered services.

Palliative care—A comprehensive approach to treating serious illness that focuses on the physical, psychological, spiritual, and existential needs of the patient—sometimes called "comfort care" or "hospice type care."

Parens Patriae—Latin for "parent of his country." Refers to the role of the state as guardian of legally disabled individuals.

Party—Person having a direct interest in a legal matter, transaction or proceeding.

Peer Review Organization (PRO)—The agencies responsible for ongoing review of the inpatient hospital care provided to people who are eligible for Medicare.

Permanent Unconsciousness—A condition that, to a reasonable degree of medical certainty: (1) will last permanently, without improvement; and (2) in which cognitive thought, sensation, purposeful action, social interaction, and awareness of self and environment are absent; and (3) which condition has existed for a period of time sufficient, in accordance with applicable professional standards, to make such a diagnosis; and (4) which condition is confirmed by a physician who is qualified and experienced in making such a diagnosis.

Person—An individual, corporation, business trust, estate, trust, partnership, association, joint venture, government, governmental subdivision or agency, or any other legal or commercial entity.

Petition—A formal written request to a court which initiates a special proceeding.

Petitioner—In a special proceeding, one who commences a formal written application, requesting some action or relief, addressed to a court for determination.

Physician—A person licensed by the state to practice medicine.

Post Mortem—Latin for "after death." Refers to the coroner's examination of a body to determine cause of death.

Power of Attorney—A legal document authorizing another to act on one's behalf.

Primary Physician—A physician designated by an individual or the individual's agent, guardian, or surrogate, to have primary responsibility for the individual's health care or, in the absence of a designation or if the designated physician is not reasonably available, a physician who undertakes the responsibility.

Procurement—The process of retrieving organs and/or tissue from a donor.

Respiratory arrest—The cessation of breathing, i.e., an event in which an individual stops breathing and if breathing is not restored, an individual's heart eventually will stop beating, resulting in cardiac arrest.

Statute—A law.

Suicide—The deliberate termination of one's existence.

Surrogate—A person designated to make health care decisions for another individual if that individual is unable to make or communicate these decisions.

Survival Statute—A statute that preserves for a decedent's estate a cause of action for infliction of pain and suffering and related damages suffered up to the moment of death.

Terminal Illness—An incurable condition caused by injury, disease or illness which, regardless of the application of life-sustaining procedures would, within reasonable medical judgment, produce death and where the application of life-sustaining procedures serve only to postpone the moment of death of the patient.

Terminally Ill Patient—A patient whose death is imminent or whose condition, to a reasonable degree of medical certainty, is hopeless unless he or she is artificially supported through the use of life-sustaining procedures and which condition is confirmed by a physician who is qualified and experienced in making such a diagnosis.

Testify—The offering of a statement in a judicial proceeding, under oath and subject to the penalty of perjury.

Testimony—The sworn statement make by a witness in a judicial proceeding.

Transplantation—The transfer of cells, tissues, or organs from an area of the body to another or from one organism to another.

Transplant Centers—Hospitals or medical centers that perform organ and/or tissue transplants.

Unconstitutional—Refers to a statute which conflicts with the United States Constitution rendering it void.

Underwrite—In insurance law, it refers to the assumption of the risk of loss to the insured's person or property, by the insurer of the insurance policy.

Uniform Laws—Laws that have been approved by the Commissioners on Uniform State Laws, and which are proposed to all state legislatures for consideration and adoption.

Waiver—An intentional and voluntary surrender of a right.

Ward—A person over whom a guardian is appointed to manage his or her affairs.

Will—A legal document which a person executes setting forth their wishes as to the distribution of their property upon death.

Withholding or Withdrawing treatment—Forgoing life-sustaining measures or discontinuing them after they have been used for a certain period of time.

Witness—One who testifies to what he has seen, heard, or otherwise observed.

X—Refers to the mark that may be used to denote one's signature when the signer is unable to write his or her name.

BIBLIOGRAPHY AND ADDITIONAL RESOURCES

The American Medical Association (Date Visited: September 2006) <http://www.ama-assn.org/>.

The Association for Responsible Medicine (Date Visited: September 2006) <http://www.a-r-m.org/>.

Black's Law Dictionary, Fifth Edition. St. Paul, MN: West Publishing Company, 1979.

Center for Medicare Advocacy (Date Visited: September 2006) <http://www.medicareadvocacy.org/>.

Centers for Disease Control (Date Visited: September 2006) <http://www.cdc.gov/.

The Federation of State Medical Boards (Date Visited: September 2006) <http://www.fsmb.org/>.

Health Care Choices (Date Visited: September 2006) <http://www.healthcarechoices.org/>.

The Hospice Patient's Alliance (Date Visited: September 2006) <http://www.hospicepatients.org/>.

National Academy of Elder Law Attorneys (Date Visited: September 2006) <http://www.naela.org/>.

National Senior Citizens Law Center (Date Visited: September 2006) <http://www.nsclc.org/>.

Social Security Administration (Date Visited: September 2006) <http://www.ssa.gov/>.

United States Department of Health (Date Visited: September 2006) <http://www.dhhs.gov/>.

United States Department of Health and Human Services Office of Disability, Aging and Long-Term Care (Date Visited: September 2006) <http://aspe.os.dhhs.gov/daltcp/home>.